HELP!
I'M LOCKED UP...
AND I NEED PEACE!

HELP!

I'M LOCKED UP...
AND I NEED PEACE!

BY
LYNN POTTER

Potter's
Heart
Ministry

Ministering God's love to the broken.

Dedication

I dedicate this work to the best anger management Coach and Friend
a person could ever have… Jesus Christ. Without Him, my life would be
nothing but a series of events with no meaning or lasting value in the great
scheme of things. Without Him, I would continue searching in vain for a
way out of the cycle of rejection, anger, rage, and hopelessness.
Without Him, life itself would be meaningless.

It is to Him…the Lover of my soul…
the One who never leaves my side…I dedicate this work.

May He be pleased with the work of His servant's hand.

Contents

Preface

Craving love and acceptance is a human desire deposited within the depths of our souls by our Creator. This craving is Divine in nature and given in order that we would pursue God with all we have. Because of the twisted way we have embraced this desire, we have become an angry society incapable of controlling our reactions to the inability of others to fulfill the emptiness it creates.

This emptiness in and of itself is not evil, but our reactions to it can be. If we take a minute and look around, we must admit that at every level of society, we find uncontrollable rage. We have even given titles like *road rage* to explain the insane actions of others. We are offended by the least little thing because mountains of unhealed soul-wounds lie deep within the space where God should reside, and we cannot contain the magnitude of it all…we become walking, breathing volcanoes ready to erupt.

This book is an attempt to provide you, the reader, with some tools to *lay an ax to the root* (Matthew 3:10) of your anger and rage, in order that you may receive healing and victory in your life. As any gardener will tell you, unless you remove the root of a plant, whatever is in the ground will eventually grow again, even if you cut it off at ground level.

We enter many of our self-help programs doing just that…cutting the thing off at ground level. We only *scratch the surface*, so to speak, not wanting to dig deep to find the root, much less grab it and yank it out. The whole process seems too overwhelming as we cannot handle the thought of touching that deep-rooted pain.

Jesus tells us in Luke 4:18 that one of the reasons God sent Him was to heal the brokenhearted and set the captives free. Even if you are not *locked up* in a physical prison, you may be *locked up* in an emotional one. This book has been written with you in mind! Jesus wants to heal you and set you free from all your emotional and spiritual sicknesses so that you can live the life He died to give you.

I encourage you to read Alex's story and engage in this workbook with this in mind...*If I let Jesus take me to the places I don't want to go, where unimaginable emotional pain and suffering reside, He will set me free from the pain, and take up residence there.*

God bless you my friend as you begin a journey that is sure to set you free...

Introduction

Hi. My name is Alex. I've been referred to as *Hudson...Inmate #624726*, by our prison system for years. Being incarcerated for most of my life, I started to believe my first name was *Hudson*, and my last name was *Inmate #624726*.

If you've had the unfortunate opportunity to call any one of our jails or prisons home for any length of time, you know what I'm talking about.

In addition to *Hudson, Inmate #624726*, I've been known to be called Snake by those who have done time with me, and have seen me in action.

It's not the most flattering name around, but I suppose it's a good fit. You see, I admit... *I am a hot-head*. One of my bunkies once said, "Hudson... you're a hissing snake ready to strike... nobody can get near you." For that reason, the addition of Snake to Inmate #624726 became part of my identity.

At first, I blew it off as a bunch of nonsense until I got locked up this last time. During my cooling-off period in booking, I thought about what he said...*you're a hissing snake...ready to strike...nobody can get near you.*

Yeah, I suppose he's right. *Wonder why I'm like that?*

Granny, who you will meet later in this book, used to say, "Alex, if you could *just* get *healing* for that *anger and rage* inside of you... you're like an active volcano ready to erupt without warning."

My buddy's explanation made more sense to me, but now, as I sit in booking for no less than the tenth time, I'm taking a serious look at Granny's.

What the h--- was she talking about? **Healing** *for* **anger** *and* **rage**???

Granny's explanations always included Jesus, God, and the Bible. I suppose that's why I never paid much attention to them. Don't get me wrong, I respected what she believed, but I just couldn't see what healing had to do with anger and rage.

I've written this book to help us both understand what she was talking about. I wrote it after I was released from prison and *still* had a *serious problem* with anger.

Even though I was a Christian and received Jesus into my life while I was in prison, I still *erupted* with **anger** and **rage** when something **triggered** me. I observed other Christians doing the same, and realized I was not alone in this struggle.

Because you have chosen to read this book, I believe you have the desire to get to the **root** of your anger. I am honored that you have chosen to do so.

During the course of this study, we will take a look at some of the events that caused me to *erupt* with anger and rage. I will introduce you to Mr. T, the owner of a Christian Publishing company, who tests my patience. You will meet Ms. Madeline and Granny who are the only stable people in my life. I will take you with me when I volunteer in our local County Prison and show you how *forgiveness sets us free*.

I offer you these small glimpses into my life, trusting you will *experience peace* as you use the truth set before you to *extinguish the volcano within*.

The Lord bless you and keep you;
The Lord make His face shine upon you,
And be gracious to you;
The Lord lift up His countenance upon you,
And give you peace.

(Numbers 6:24-26)

CHAPTER 1
The Offense and the Volcano

MR. T's Publishing House

"You can't be serious!"

I pound my fist on the desk and watch the man's glass of water shake. He doesn't budge. This makes me angrier. *"NOT SUITABLE MATERIAL...EH?"* I'm up in a flash leaning across his desk. My intent is to be *in his face*. Yeah, close enough for him to smell the onions and salami I had on my pizza for lunch.

"Alex, please..."

"I'm sorry Ms. Madeline, but this guy is nuts...*Not suitable material?*" I turn to this incredibly offensive person and start sizing him up. I'm pretty good at that.

As many years as I've spent locked up...well...let's just say I've had lots of experience. It was all part of survival, you see. You had to be able to spot your opponent's weakness and *respond... like...right now* in order to stay alive and on top of things.

Anyhow, survival mode kicks in and I scan him like a brand new printer; quick and thorough. I finish my lightning speed assessment and find him seriously lacking...

He's just...well...clueless.

He sits behind his mammoth desk like he's in the Oval Office or something. I'd like to *throw something* at his stone-cold face just to see if it would crack. He's dressed in a three piece black suit with a stiff, perfectly pressed white shirt that looks like it would crack if he ever tried to move.

Gold cufflinks shine as he stretches his hand toward me. And...oh well...the shirt sleeves don't crack and fall to pieces on the mammoth desk. Too bad...how fun it would be if his finely starched shirt sleeves shattered, releasing the golden cufflinks, and they rolled off the desk and onto the floor. I would then have the satisfaction of slowly crushing them before I slammed the door in his face on my way out...I can hear them crunch now. *Man! I get off just thinking about it.*

Oh...well...I'm sorry...but...

No, I guess I'm not sorry. Not really. I cringe at everything about him...ugh...I'm surprised he doesn't have a red hanky dangling out of one of those finely pressed suit pockets...

Stiff clothes...*stiff* face...*stiff* person...

I'm tempted to look under the desk. If I were still in <u>The County</u>, I'd be passing around small pieces of paper for my fellow inmates to place their bets on the shoes. *My* money is on shiny, pointed, *stiff*, designer shoes.

I can't help myself. I lean back in defiance, refusing the handshake that is attached to the gold cufflinks and three piece suit. For a brief moment I stare at him with hardcore contempt. Temptation to do the wrong thing is waving its dark beauty before me like the night I took my first hit of crack in crazy Hillbilly's barn.

The *old Alex* is begging to re-surface and cave in to the sweet desire...to crawl under the desk, and no matter what kind of shoes they are, work up something real nasty, and spit on them. Let me tell you...*old Alex* is always lurking around the corner waiting to snatch up an opportunity to make a fool out of me, and if possible, get me into trouble.

He almost wins this time. If it weren't for Ms. Madeline whining, *"PLEASE...Alex! PLEASE!"* and visions of Granny crying at the foot of her bed begging her God to do something with me (like save my sorry fanny) I'd already be under the desk.

Well, better not go there. It just ain't Christian-like. *But...man...would it feel good.* My blood's boiling but I am maintaining control. At Ms. Madeline's whining, I pull back and sit.

The man still does not budge. He shuffles through our papers and mumbles. This causes me to churn inside. I want to grab him and shake him. *What's wrong with you?* I rub my wet palms on my knees, waiting.

"Mr. Hudson. As I tried to tell you before your little outburst," (Light dances off the shiny cufflinks as he lifts his arm to pull off his designer glasses.) "This is not suitable material for our publishing company to print. There is too much graphic explanation of...how do I say it... *issues of life*. We have a very sensitive readership and do not believe this material would sell. Frankly, it borders on risqué."

Now, I hate it when people use words I don't understand, especially when they are *rejecting* me. Risque' sounds *really bad* and I look to Ms. Madeline for help.

"Off-color, or indecent, Alex." she says and lowers her head. I figure she's just waiting for me to blow. I'm getting real close and want to make sure whatever I say will hit the mark and make this guy think. Like I said before...*He's clueless*.

I look at Ms. Madeline and know she is praying her head off. It is our fifth meeting in a week and she knows I am getting tired of the rejection. *Why don't they GET IT?* I just don't understand. It's not like we are writing anything different than what they read about on Sunday mornings...

Or...is it?

I'm thankful for Ms. Madeline's silent praying because I know it will keep me from doing something really crazy in here. But, I also know I'm too far over the other side of this one to keep my mouth shut. **I'm at the boiling point now, and I'm ready to release some steam.**

I look at Ms. Madeline and *rise slowly for a dramatic effect*. Then, I spin around once and plant my hands on his desk...hard. His water glass jumps again. I lean forward, clench my fists, and pound harder. I have accomplished my *in your face* stance and shout...

"You arrogant, self-righteous, money- hungry S.O.B." (I'm sure he can smell the onions and salami now.) He backs away. Out of the corner of my eye, I see Ms. Madeline flinch. She gets up and comes toward me.

"Alex...don't."

"Too late Ms. Madeline." I say. "Granny taught me to stand up for what I believe. I thought when we came to these kinds of places we'd get some respect for what we're doing. Guess I was wrong. I've listened to all their B.S. and *I've had it*. I'm going to stand up *right now* for what I believe.

I'm going to stand up for every man, woman, and child who the system has *locked up*. I'm going to stand up for their rights as people; people who need help getting back into society, back into healthy relationships, and back into life.

We know the truth, Ms. Madeline, but all these self-righteous cats we've been wasting our time with don't. They say they do, but they *don't*. They're full of smoke, just like a fire that is about to burn out. Just smoke...just a bunch of B.S. smoke!!!"

Ms. Madeline's got me by my arm trying to escort me out of the man's office before I become completely unglued. She knows me. She knows when I'm about to erupt with some language that I'll regret later. She can't contain me, and in my rage, I bump into a plant stand and the plant falls to the floor shattering the pot.

The man stands and comes toward me. I pick up a piece of the shattered pot and raise it into the air. "Don't even...don't even *think* of coming near me." The man stops and I continue, "Do you see this? Do you see what happened? Do you have any idea what this signifies?"

"You...you in your self-righteous ivory tower with mahogany furniture, waterfalls, plants, and stained glass windows...*you haven't a clue*." I point toward the window behind his desk. "You have *no idea* what's going on out there in the real world, far as I can tell. You *ever* taken the time to notice *anything?* Or do you just walk on by; turning your head, afraid you'll get dirty brushing up against some risqué-type people?" I'm still clutching the piece of clay. "*Well?*" I don't give him a chance to answer.

"Have you ever read the Book you say you believe? Do you know what kind of people are in that Book? Do you know what kind of person wrote a bunch of the Psalms? Do you know what the Apostle Paul said about himself? How about Ammon and Tamar, what about David and Bathsheba? Just take a look at Jesus' ancestors and study some of their *lives!!!*"

"You are clueless, my man, you are *SO* clueless."

"They were all pots. All broken pots just like this piece I have in my hand. Let me tell you something, you simple imp! If it weren't for stuff like what we're trying to get you to publish, I can *guarantee* you I wouldn't be standing here holding this piece... *I'd be coming at your throat with it.*"

Rage is overtaking all my sense of respect. I cannot contain it. Words are shooting out of my mouth like a machine gun and I can't stop. I'm sure some of what I am saying is true, but the attitude behind the words is bad, I mean...*really bad.*

Ms. Madeline is begging me to leave. The man opens his mouth and attempts to speak. I hold my hand up. "Don't even start...there's nothing you have to say I want to hear." I cut him off.

I remember a perfectly positioned Bible lying on a fancy table by the door. We passed it on the way in. I wonder if *anyone* has *ever* read it. I wonder if the pages would stick together if I tried to turn them.

I walk over, pick it up, and wave it in the air.

"Mister, if you are representing what is in this Book, I suggest *very strongly* you *READ* it, OK??? You might *just* find some people you wouldn't want to be seen with and stuff happening in there that is *not suitable for your readership!!!*"

Ms. Madeline has me half way out the door by now. Even though I am still hot and waving my arms around like a wild man, I stop long enough to place the tidy Bible back on the tidy table.

I am rewarded with great satisfaction as I notice his stunned expression. I loose myself from Ms. Madeline's grip and reach for the door. Before I slam it in his face, I watch him pick up the Bible. Our eyes lock and...

There's no doubt in my mind that we'll meet again...

CHAPTER 1 REFLECTION
The Offense and the Volcano

Well, there you have it. Alex Hudson, the reformed jailbird going ballistic on the owner of a *Christian* publishing company. What do you think of that? I *think* I'm not too proud of myself and need help **extinguishing** this **raging volcano** inside of me. Maybe you have some thoughts that will help...

What do you think made me *so angry?*

_____

_____

_____

What do you think I was struggling with in Mr. T's office? (Hint-old Alex acting out)

_____

_____

_____

Why was I struggling? (What do you think *triggered* my anger?)

_____

_____

_____

How about you?

Why did you get angry? (Think about a time you got angry and what happened.)

Write about it on the following lines:

_____

_____

_____

_____

_____

What were you struggling with? (What do *you* think caused you to get *angry?*)

_____

_____

_____

_____

_____

_____

Why were you struggling? (What do you think might have *triggered* your anger?)

_____

_____

_____

_____

_____

_____

Granny sent me a poem when I was locked up once, and I want to share it with you. Take a minute to meditate on the words and journal your thoughts on the lines following the poem. Try writing *your own* poem or essay about *your* experiences with anger. Writing helps me process stuff that happens to me and sets me free by helping me get honest with myself and the situation. Give it a try!

Anger Defined:

My tender heart crushed like a red petal
Bleeding in the dark...
Emerges from the depths
In a fit of rage

Who can know me
But by what they see or hear?

Is it really me?
Or someone I've created

In order to survive?

By Lynn Potter 8/4/08

MY THOUGHTS ON MS. LYNN'S POEM ON ANGER.....MY POEM ABOUT ANGER:

_____

_____

_____

_____

_____

_____

_____

_____

_____

_____

_____

_____

_____

_____

I read Ms. Lynn's poem often. It's opened my eyes to the fact that anger is **_the result_** of **_something else_** that's going on **_inside_** of me.

I received the following letter from Granny when I was in _lock down_ at _The County_ because I _went off_ on one of my fellow inmates and started a fight. It got me to thinking about where I was, how I got there, and where I was headed if something didn't change.

Think about a recent situation where you got _angry_ and _went off_ as you read...

My dear Alex,

You've **got** to get to the **root** of your outbursts or you'll never be free. Stuff has happened in your life that you haven't dealt with and the end result is always the same. You go off on the wrong person or do some crazy thing...and poof...before you know it you're back in handcuffs heading off to the nearest jail or prison. And, it doesn't stop there. You get **locked down** while you're **locked up** because you can't seem to control the rage inside of you. You're like a sleeping volcano ready to erupt without warning.

It's not necessarily what's going on in the present that causes you to act like you do. You've had a tough life, Alex. Your parents didn't know how to love you and deserted you when you were young. You had no family, so you started hanging out on street corners and dope houses, and un-

speakable things were done to you. You were always on the run trying to forget in a haze of make-believe that was induced by the latest drug or booze. You act hard and clench your fists ready to fight anyone who looks at you sideways, while all the while you are still a little kid crying out in the dark for true love.

I took you in after your parents were gone, but you were so wounded you couldn't receive my love. Maybe you just didn't know how. Many a night I waited up for you and heard you come staggering in. No matter how high or drunk you got, it never seemed to ease your pain. Even now, my heart aches as I remember hearing the bed creek as you flopped down on it and cried yourself to sleep.

The next morning you'd be red-eyed, holding your stomach, and hollering for my biscuits 'n gravy like nothing ever happened. You stunk to high heaven of rot-gut booze and cheap cologne. You'd look around dazed and confused, hoping I wouldn't notice how hung over you were. My heart broke for you because I was powerless to take away your pain. Over the years I've come to realize that only God can heal your broken heart.

It's time to stop covering everything up with drugs and booze and bad relationships. It's time to stop running...

You need help, Alex, and there's only one Person who can help you. I know how you hate people preaching at you, and don't worry, I'm not about to start. But, please Alex, there's nowhere else for you to turn. You've tried everything and nothing works. You always end up back where you started or worse every time.

It's time to stop covering everything up with drugs and booze and bad relationships. It's time to stop running, and sit still long enough to get some help before it's too late. You've got to make the decision, Alex.

THE CHOICE IS YOURS....

When you're ready to face the reality of your past and how it is affecting you now, I'm here for you. It's the only way out of this viscous cycle, Alex. The way I see it, there's a broken heart under all that anger that needs to be healed. I'm attaching a worksheet I did for one of my books. I titled it, "Help for the Hurting Heart." I think it will help you begin the process of understanding yourself and why you can't control your anger.

As always...all my love,
Granny

HELP FOR THE HURTING HEART
BY GRANNY G.

The first step to healing of any kind is to admit we have a problem. Whether it is physical, emotional, or spiritual, unless we recognize our need for healing, we will not seek help, and continue to live life *acting out* of our brokenness.

Most of us would go to a doctor if we had a broken leg or foot. It's very hard and painful to walk with either one. Trust me, I know. Anyhow, the doctor more than likely would order some X-rays to see where the fracture or break originated and how severe the wound was. Then he or she would be able to determine the best course of action to help the broken bone heal.

It is the same with a broken heart. A broken heart will cause emotional and spiritual sickness which results in the inability to *walk* through life as a *whole* and *healthy* person. ***Acting out*** of a ***broken heart*** causes harm to ourselves and those around us.

The heart is the center of our being from which all our actions find their root. Take a minute to think about the emotions, actions, and reactions you have experienced over the course of your life. Whether they are good or bad, they have all originated from the ***condition of your heart***.

If your heart is *healthy*, you will walk in love, peace, joy, and all the fruit *of the spirit*. If it is *unhealthy*, you will experience anger, hate, rage, outbursts of wrath, jealousy, envy, and all the works *of the flesh*.

Read Galatians 5:19-25 below and think about ***your heart's condition*** as you read. Is your heart healthy or unhealthy? Remember, evidence of a *healthy heart* is walking in the *fruit of the spirit*. Evidence of an *unhealthy heart* is a life dictated by the *works of the flesh*.

Galatians 5:19-25: (NKJV)

Now the *works of the flesh* are evident, which are: adultery, fornication, uncleanness, lewdness, idolatry, sorcery, hatred, contentions, jealousies, outbursts of wrath, selfish ambitions, dissensions, heresies, envy, murders, drunkenness, revelries, and the like; of which I tell you beforehand, just as I also told you in time past, that those who practice such things will not inherit the kingdom of God.

But the *fruit of the Spirit* is love, joy, peace, longsuffering, kindness, goodness, faithfulness, gentleness, self-control. Against such there is no law. And those who are Christ's have crucified the flesh with its passions and desires. If we live in the Spirit, let us also walk in the Spirit.

Next…let's read Galatians 5:19-25 from the *Life Recovery Bible*…

When you follow the desires of your sinful nature, the results are very clear: sexual immorality, impurity, lustful pleasures, idolatry, sorcery, hostility, quarreling, jealousy, outbursts of anger, selfish ambition, dissension, division, envy, drunkenness, wild parties, and other sins like these. Let me tell you again, as I have before, that anyone living that sort of life will not inherit the Kingdom of God.

But the Holy Spirit produces this kind of fruit in our lives: love, joy, peace, patience, kindness, goodness, faithfulness, gentleness, and self-control. There is no law against these things!

Take a minute to re-read and circle those things above in Galatians 5:19-25 that you recognize as evident in your life.

The evidence of a *healthy heart* is one that walks in the *fruit of the spirit*.

The evidence of *an unhealthy heart* is a life dictated by the *works of the flesh*.

After taking a look at the things you circled in Galatians 5:19-25, make an honest declaration of your *heart's condition* below and give your reasons for it:

I believe the *condition of my heart* is:

_____ Healthy
_____ Unhealthy
_____ A mixture of healthy and unhealthy

Because:

_____

_____

_____

_____

_____

Read the following verses, write them out on the lines below them, and explain in your own words what they mean:

Keep your heart with all diligence, for out of it spring the issues of life. Proverbs 4:23 (NKJV) Guard your heart above all else, for it determines the course of your life. Proverbs 4:23 (Life Recovery Bible)

_____

_____

_____

_____

As a face is reflected in water, so the heart reflects the real person. Proverbs 27:19 (Life Recovery Bible.)

_____

_____

_____

_____

Jesus often taught in parables. A parable is a story told in order to explain a spiritual truth. Read the following parable. What is Jesus saying to *you* about *your* life through this parable? Write your thoughts out on the lines provided.

Do you not yet understand that whatever enters the mouth goes into the stomach and is eliminated? But those things which proceed out of the mouth come from the heart, and they defile a man. For out of the heart proceed evil thoughts, murders, adulteries, fornications, thefts, false witness, blasphemies. These are the things which defile a man, but to eat with unwashed hands does not defile a man. (Matthew 15:17-20)

I believe Jesus is telling me:

_____

_____

_____

We can try to control our anger by anger management and that is a positive thing to do. But, _unless we get to the **root** of **why** we get angry_, we will struggle with uncontrollable outbursts that cause us embarrassment, broken relationships, criminal activity, or worse.

In the above verses, the Bible says what comes out of our mouths is actually what is in our hearts. ***Simply put, anger is the result of an unhealthy heart.***

Personal notes:

_____

_____

_____

_____

_____

_____

_____

_____

_____

_____

_____

_____

_____

CHAPTER 2
Our Greatest Need

As I re-examine my *volcanic outburst* in Mr. T's Publishing office, I recognize a pattern that I seem to struggle with. He was not only *rejecting* me and what I was trying to get him to do, but he was also *rejecting* Granny, who I love dearly. He said her material was *not suitable*. So, in my heart, I felt he *rejected* me, and *he rejected Granny*. My *unhealthy heart* lied to me and said, "*You're not good enough, Granny's not good enough, and this guy's a jerk. Lash out at him and you'll feel better.*" (My thoughts were not that clean, but you get the idea!!!)

The <u>root</u> of my volcanic outburst (anger and rage) was <u>rejection</u>.

Granny taught me that *rejection* is one of mankind's most harmful experiences. She told me because we are created to experience good relationships with God and each other, we crave love and acceptance. She said this was a holy craving until sin entered the picture and everything got distorted; the perfect relationship with God was broken, and relationships between human beings fell into disarray.

"Just think about this Alex," she said. "When babies are born and first come into the world, they reach their arms out and look around. Why do you think they do that? My take on it is that they enter the world immediately craving love and acceptance. We never stop craving it no matter how old we are. We continually reach out our arms and look around for love and acceptance.

When this craving is lacking, or worse, being tampered with through mental, physical, or sexual abuse, we succumb to a prison of our own design in order to protect ourselves and survive.

Anger, rage, outbursts of profanity, drug and alcohol abuse, sexual promiscuity, stealing, cheating, lying, and all sorts of criminal activity are things that surface as we *respond to rejection* out of our *self-made prisons* of *anger* and *rage…*"

Granny was right. I was so wounded from rejection that I had a hard time developing healthy relationships and living a productive, healthy life. Drugs, alcohol, sex, and all that goes with that territory became my self-made prison. I used these destructive things to build walls around my heart in order to protect myself, but I didn't realize what I was doing. I was actually *locking myself up* in a prison full of *uncontrollable anger and rage*.

I became a volcano ready to erupt at any time without warning.

Do you remember the poem Granny shared with me? Let's re-read it:

Anger Defined:

My tender heart crushed like a red petal
Bleeding in the dark
Emerges from the depths
In a fit of rage

Who can know me
But by what they see or hear?

Is it really me?
Or someone I've created

In order to survive?

How about you? Are you a volcano ready to erupt at any time without warning? Are you ready to deal with some of the things that have caused you to build your own *heart's prison*? Are you ready to get to the **root** of your *anger*?

Are you ready to expose the volcano within for what it is?

You may have carried some of these things for years and your walls are thick. You may be afraid to face this stuff head on. You need not be afraid because *Jesus knows exactly how you feel.*

The Bible says He was *despised* and *rejected*. All His friends *deserted Him* when *He needed them the most*. He was *lied about* in a court of law. He was *unjustly condemned* and *sentenced to death*. He was *brutally beaten, nailed to a tree, and left for dead*. People *laughed at Him, ridiculed Him,* and *spit on Him*.

THERE IS NOTHING YOU HAVE GONE THROUGH THAT HE HASN'T.
HE KNOWS EXACTLY HOW YOU FEEL.   HE CAN BE TRUSTED.

Are you ready to *trust Him* with the *deepest scars* of your life? Are you ready to trust Him to *heal you* and *set you free* from the wounds you have carried for years?

Granny used to tell me…

"Alex, you got things all backwards. You're trying to live life and do the right thing all on your own. You're like a hamster stuck in a cage running in a wheel getting nowhere, and at the end of the day, your head's spinning and you're exhausted.

Aren't you tired of doing that? When are you going to realize you can't do this thing on your own? I know you hate preaching, but sometimes it's the only way to get through to you.

How many more nights do you want to spend in jail? How many more days do you want to wake up not remembering what you did the night before? How many more times do you want to face a judge trembling inside, having to fake you've got it all together?

How many more times…Alex?

You've got to come to grips with where you are and where you are headed if things don't change. ***You've got to admit you need help.***

This is where God comes in, Alex. He wants to help you get back on track and help you make something out of your life. He has a plan for your life, but you'll never know what it is until you develop a relationship with Him. That's your greatest need right now, Alex. ***YOU NEED GOD…*** ***You need God in your life!***

I'd be thrilled if you quit running around doing drugs, drinking, and having sex with anyone you meet. I'd be ecstatic if you stayed in school and graduated. I'd be real proud if you got a job and kept it for more than two weeks. Yes…Alex…all this stuff would be great and make me happy.

But...without God in your life... it will never stick...you'll always end up being that hamster spinning on that wheel.

<u>God has so much more for you, Alex, than you've experienced</u>. *Why don't you trust Him to do what He says He will do? The Bible says He can't lie. He's done everything for you already. He's sent Jesus to take the punishment for all the stuff you've done. He's paid the price so you can go free. Jesus died and rose from the dead proving He has power over everything.*

Just think about it, Alex. If Jesus has power over death, don't you think He has power over crack, booze, heroin, pot, or anything else we struggle with? Death is the ultimate rip-off in this life and Jesus has conquered it! He rose from the dead, and we can trust His ability to help us deal with anything that comes our way.

<u>Our greatest need in life is to live in relationship with God</u>. *That was impossible after sin entered the picture long ago with Adam and Eve...that is...until Jesus came along... Alex...**YOU NEED GOD!***

THAT'S YOUR NUMBER ONE PROBLEM...ALEX...YOU NEED GOD!

And guess what...Jesus will take you to Him!!!"

Long ago, Jesus said, "I am the way, the truth, and the life. No one comes to the Father except through me." (John 14:6) Write it out below:

_____

_____

"It's not that hard, Alex. It's all about faith. It's not about what you can do to prove to God that you are worthy of His attention. It's not about cleaning yourself up in order to be acceptable to Him.

It's all about coming to Him through Jesus and admitting you are a mess and you need help. It's about admitting you are a sinner and without Him there is no way you can save yourself.

It's about believing Jesus when He says you can't get to God without Him and believing He died in your place. It's about believing God raised Him from the dead.

It's nothing about you or me, Alex, it's all about Him!"

Read the following verses and write them out. What do the words mean to you?

If we confess our sins, He is faithful and just to forgive us our sins and to cleanse us from all unrighteousness. 1 John 1:9

But as many as received Him, to them He gave the right to become children of God, to those who believe in His name. John 1:12

I *finally* got it, my friend! Granny's persistent love and teaching *finally* got through to me…

It wasn't about me cleaning myself up. It wasn't about me trying to do the right thing in my own strength. It was all about Him and what he had already done for me.

Once I realized that, it was a no-brainer. I went *running* to Jesus and asked Him to be part of my life. I asked Him to take control and help me be the person He created me to be. I asked Him to forgive me for all the destructive, self-serving stuff I'd been involved in and help me apologize to everyone I'd hurt along the way.

I told Him I believe He is the Son of God Who came to earth to die in my place, carrying my sin to His cross. I told Him I believe He rose from the dead and asked Him to bring me into His family and make me His child.

I thanked Him for loving me, saving me, and setting me free to be His spokesman wherever I go. And, because you are reading this book, I know He wants me to give you the opportunity to do what I did. I am praying for you as I write this knowing God is calling you to Himself right now. His heart is for you. He wants to help you and set you free. He wants to be part of your life. He loves you and cares for you. He is not mad at you or out to get you. His desire is for you to come to Him…***right now***.

Like Granny told me…I'm telling you…we need God to survive…WE NEED GOD!

I'll write a prayer out here that you may want to use or you can create your own. In any case, **don't wait**. Do it now. **God is calling you**. You are *special* to Him. He wants **today** to be your day of salvation, your day of *freedom*. **RIGHT NOW!**

He wants you to say,

"Today is the beginning of a new life for me because Jesus has saved me, set me free, and I am God's child."

Dear Jesus,

I come to You asking forgiveness for my sin. I believe the Bible is true and when it says if I confess my sin, You are faithful and just to forgive me, and You are faithful and just to cleanse me. Thank You, Jesus for saving me, forgiving me, and cleansing me of my sin. I believe You are the Son of God, that You were crucified in my place, and that You died and rose again. I believe You are seated at the right hand of God making intercession for me. I believe the Bible when it says I am Your child. I thank You for bringing me into Your family, and I ask You to help me to live my life following You and Your ways. Please bring people into my life who will help me learn more about You, and help me to live the Christian life.

I thank You…Jesus…that today_____is my spiritual birthday.

If you would like to write your own prayer, I would encourage you to do so on the following lines. GOD BLESS YOU! THIS IS YOUR SPIRITUAL BIRTHDAY!!!

_____

_____

_____

_____

_____

_____

CHAPTER 3
Critical Choices

Congrats and Happy Spiritual Birthday! I believe you've either given your life to Jesus for the first time, or you've rededicated your life to Him. Awesome stuff either way, my friend! Let's follow Him together as He shows us the way to a new kind of life; a life that's full of **PEACE** and contentment instead of anger and rage.

So far, we've taken time to examine my outburst in Mr. T's Publishing office. I've given you an opportunity to examine your life and your issues with *anger*. We have discussed that one of the *root causes* of our *anger* is *rejection*.

In this application section we'll take a look at Jesus' life and examine some of the ways He experienced *rejection*. We'll discover that we're not alone in our suffering.

Granny said *rejection* is one of life's *most wounding experiences*. Write about an experience where you feel you have been *wounded* by *rejection* on the following lines. We will use it to help you receive healing from the *rejection* and find *freedom* from re-occurring *anger* and *rage out-bursts*. Use extra paper if needed.

_____

_____

_____

_____

_____

_____

_____

_____

_____

_____

_____

Emotional pain can cause *twisted thinking*. If we do not process *emotional pain* Jesus' way, we will believe the *lie* that we are alone and no one understands or cares.

Read the following verses and write them out on the lines provided. Explain in your own words what they mean. Both verses are talking about Jesus.

Therefore, it was necessary for him to be made in every respect like us, his brothers and sisters, so that he could be our merciful and faithful High Priest before God. Then he could offer a sacrifice that would take away the sins of the people. Since he himself has gone through suffering and testing, he is able to help us when we are being tested. Hebrews 2:17-18 (Life Recovery Bible)

Verse:

_____

_____

_____

_____

_____

My interpretation:

_____

_____

_____

_____

_____

_____

So then, since we have a great High Priest who has entered heaven, Jesus the Son of God, let us hold firmly to what we believe. This High Priest of ours understands our weaknesses, for he faced all of the same testings we do, yet he did not sin. So let us come boldly to the throne of our gracious God. There we will receive his mercy, and we will find grace to help us when we need it most. Hebrews 4:14-16 (Life Recovery Bible.)

Verse:

_____

_____

_____

_____

_____

My interpretation:

_____

_____

_____

_____

These two verses in Hebrews help us understand we are never alone in our suffering. They tell us about Jesus and how He can relate to everything we go through.

Granny had to fetch me out of jail one night after I got into a fight over something lame and was slapped with a public drunkenness, disorderly conduct, and intent to do bodily harm charge. (Yeah…now that's a mouthful!) Anyhow, she was none too happy because they called her in the middle of some big church dinner, and she had to tell her friends where I was...once again.

After she poured me into the front seat, she said, _"Alex… You've got to get something settled. You can't go on lashing out at everyone who looks at you sideways. You've got to take a look at what triggers your anger and find the root cause for your insane actions. You've got to take responsibility and find out how to stop this destructive behavior._

I've heard you say more than once you can't help how you feel and that nobody understands what you are going through. You've even told me to my face that nobody cares about you, knowing it was a bold-faced lie. You were talking to the one person on this earth who does love you and has shown it every day of your life! Even if you had no one on this earth, you have Jesus. He loves you more than I ever could, more perfectly than anyone ever would, and He never stops loving you. Even when you're running around acting crazy, He loves you. Even when you turn your back on Him, He loves you. Even when you can't stand yourself, He loves you!

He's experienced everything you have gone through, are going through, and will go through. **It's entirely up to you whether or not you invite him into your space.**

Don't believe the lie that no one understands or cares!! It's simply not true…

I know you love a challenge. Some of our best conversations have been when you've tried to prove me wrong. I challenge you to prove me wrong on this, Alex. I challenge you to read about Jesus and examine His life. Then come back to me and tell me no one understands. Won't happen…my young friend….I promise you.

You'll end up having to suck it up and admit that someone does understand and cares. You'll have to suck it up and **make the choice** to overcome your anger and rage with His help."

We pulled into the driveway and it couldn't have been soon enough for me. "Granny..." I said. "I don't mean no disrespect or nothin', but can't we talk about this tomorrow? I appreciate you comin' for me and all, but my head is pounding and I just want to crash."

"Alex, I'll never stop prayin'. I'll never stop believing. The Good Lord's going to get hold of you one day and make something out of your life. You wait and see..."

I suspect Granny stayed on her knees at the foot of her bed that night because one day I started taking a close look at my life. Why did petty, nit-picky stuff bug me to the point of uncontrollable rage? I justified every outburst and insane reaction as I remembered them. People disappointed me, they turned their backs on me, lied to me, used me, stole from me, took advantage of me...and...I mean...took advantage of me bad! I had every **right** to go off...didn't I?

Was Granny right? Was I living life in a self-made prison of solitary confinement crying out for love?

Was Granny right? Was I living life in a self-made prison of solitary confinement crying out for love? Do I lash out in order to protect some wounded little kid inside? Am I using drugs, booze, and bad relationships to hide the true me?

I can laugh or seem brave and have it all together as long as my mind is controlled by some artificial high, *but inside I am crawling with rage fueled by rejection.* As long as I cover it up with artificial laughter and mind-controlling substances, I look like I have it all together and *actually start believing it myself.*

What about you? Are you hiding behind mind-altering substances, artificial highs, and bad relationships? Are you struggling with keeping it together? Has your anger and rage made life unmanageable for you and those around you? Have you ever been like me, and found yourself locked up because of your inability to control your anger?

***Are you living life out of a self-made prison of
solitary confinement crying out for love?***

What part has anger or rage played in causing you to get locked up in a physical, emotional, or spiritual prison?

_____

_____

_____

_____

Granny challenged me because she knows how I like to prove people wrong. I took her up on it because, to be honest, I thought it was a crock…all this mumbo-jumbo about God. I slammed the door shut after she challenged me that night and staggered up the stairs to my room. I was royally ticked off, but not at her. So…who was I ticked off at anyhow?

The next morning, while nursing a whopper of a hangover, I was lured into the kitchen by the inviting aroma of biscuits n' gravy. I found Granny at the stove preparing my *morning after* meal. She brought me a plate, and, without a word, sat it in front of me.

I knew better than to say anything but, "Thank you Granny, thank you."

She left me alone to go tend to her flowers and vegetable garden. Granny found peace tending to her plants, especially when I've done something to upset her. I sat at the table holding my pounding head wondering why I keep doing what I do.

Out of nowhere Granny shows up holding a Bible. She hands it to me and says, "Alex…here…I bought this for you last week. I meant it about that challenge I gave you." She lays the book in front of me and lightly taps the cover. "Read it sometime when you're head's not pounding… might just do you some good."

What could I say after I put her through another trip to fetch me out of jail? "Ok. Granny, I promise." I said.

She hands me a manila envelope with the Bible and says, "I wrote a worksheet on *critical choices*, and I want you to do it using this here Bible I bought you. When you're done, we'll talk." Now, if you know Granny, this was not a suggestion, it was a command! I'm going to share it with you now. It's…well…you'll see…

CRITICAL CHOICES
BY GRANNY G.

Let's begin by reading Matthew 1:18-19 as it is written in The Life Recovery Bible:

This is how Jesus the Messiah was born. His mother, Mary, was engaged to be married to Joseph. But before the marriage took place, while she was still a virgin, she became pregnant through the power of the Holy Spirit. Joseph, her fiancé, was a good man and did not want to disgrace her publicly, so he decided to break the engagement quietly.

Read Matthew 1:18-19 again and write your thoughts out on the lines provided.   Explain how this situation could cause Jesus to experience rejection:

_____

_____

_____

From the get-go Jesus experienced *rejection*. He was considered illegitimate; His mother was pregnant before she got married. Society did not look favorably on unwed mothers. They were considered the scum of the earth, unclean, and despised. And…children of unwed mothers were just as despised.

Next, let's read Luke 2:1-7:

And it came to pass in those days that a decree went out from Caesar Augustus that all the world should be registered. This census first took place while Quirinius was governing Syria. So all went to be registered, everyone to his own city. Joseph also went up from Galilee, out of the city of Nazareth, into Judea, to the city of David, which is called Bethlehem, because he was of the house and lineage of David, to be registered with Mary, his betrothed wife, who was with child. So it was, that while they were there, the days were completed for her to be delivered. And she brought forth her firstborn Son, and wrapped Him in swaddling clothes, and laid Him in a manger, because there was no room for them in the inn.

What we've just read brings us to the conclusion that Joseph did, in fact, stay with Mary, and she was just about to give birth when they finished their trip from Nazareth to Bethlehem.

Jesus was *rejected* again *before* He was born. We are told there was **no room for them in the inn**. Was it because the hotels were full due to the census? Or, could it have been because gossip travels quickly, and Mary was recognized as one of *those women*?

At any rate, there were no accommodations made for a pregnant woman about to give birth, and Jesus had to spend His first minutes of life wrapped up lying in a *feeding trough*!

Yeah, I said a *feeding trough*…most likely it was a carved out rock where people threw slop in to feed their animals. Did you know that is what a *manger* is? It was not a quaint little crib like we see on Christmas cards. It was a *feeding trough* for animals that probably had to been cleaned out before they put Him in it.

But…that's nothing compared to what happens to Him next…

Read Matthew 2:1-14 from the Life Recovery Bible:

Jesus was born in Bethlehem in Judea, during the reign of King Herod. About that time some wise men from eastern lands arrived in Jerusalem, asking, "Where is the newborn king of the Jews? We saw his star as it rose, and we have come to worship him."

King Herod was deeply disturbed when he heard this, as was everyone in Jerusalem. He called a meeting of the leading priests and teachers of religious law and asked, "Where is the Messiah supposed to be born?"

"In Bethlehem in Judea," they said, "for this is what the prophet wrote:

> **'And you, O Bethlehem in the land of Judah,**
> **are not least among the ruling cities of Judah,**
> **for a ruler will come from you**
> **who will be the shepherd for my people Israel.' "**

Then Herod called for a private meeting with the wise men, and he learned from them the time when the star first appeared. Then he told them, "Go to Bethlehem and search carefully for the child. And when you find him, come back and tell me so that I can go and worship him, too!"

After this interview the wise men went their way. And the star they had seen in the east guided them to Bethlehem. It went ahead of them and stopped over the place where the child was. When they saw the star, they were filled with joy! They entered the house and saw the child with his mother, Mary, and they bowed down and worshiped him. Then they opened their treasure chests and gave him gifts of gold, frankincense, and myrrh.

When it was time to leave, they returned to their own country by another route, for God had warned them in a dream not to return to Herod.

After the wise men were gone, an angel of the Lord appeared to Joseph in a dream. "Get up! Flee to Egypt with the child and his mother," the angel said. "Stay there until I tell you to return, because Herod is going to search for the child to kill him."

That night Joseph left for Egypt with the child and Mary, his mother, and they stayed there until Herod's death. This fulfilled what the Lord had spoken through the prophet: I called my Son out of Egypt.

Jesus is pegged as illegitimate, He's despised and rejected, some crazy old king wants to kill Him, and His family is on the run.

What a story! What drama! The Bible tells us there was a king named Herod who was furious when he heard there was a kid who was being called *King of the Jews*. This demented king lied to some astrologers (Wise Men) in order to track this small child down to get rid of Him... to kill Him.

Pretty crazy...right? Some king jealous of a little kid...jealous to the point of murder? Yeah...I thought so. There must be something pretty special about this kid because Joseph has another dream with an angel talking to him. The angel tells him to get out of town and do it...like... *NOW*!

So, now Jesus, his mother, and Joseph are on the run. The Bible doesn't tell us exactly how old Jesus is at the time; it just says He was a *young Child*. What we've learned about Him so far is: He's pegged as illegitimate, He's despised and rejected, some crazy old king wants to kill Him, and His family is on the run.

What a way to start life!

Not exactly the perfect environment to grow up and become a productive member of society, is it? Not exactly the perfect environment to develop a *healthy heart*, is it?

I don't know about you, but after reading this much of Jesus' story, *I have to admit* that He understands what it's like to *experience rejection*, even at a very young age! Granny sure made her point, didn't she?

So...where does all this knowledge leave us?

It demands we respond to Granny's challenge!

We have some <u>choices</u> to make. We can choose to believe what we read. We can choose to take what we've learned and let the information sink in. We can choose to believe Jesus understands our pain.

We can choose to believe the more we read about His life, the more we will realize He is able and willing to help us process our rejection, and give us victory over our anger and rage. We can choose to believe or not. It is our choice.

We have the free will to choose. Today we must choose! What'll it be???

I, Alex, *choose* this day to believe what I read. I, Alex, *choose* this day to take what I've learned about Jesus and let it sink in. I, Alex, *choose* this day to believe Jesus understands my pain, is able and willing to help me process my pain caused by rejection, and give me victory over my anger and rage.

I, <u>Alex</u>, choose this day to believe.

How about you? Will you follow me as I respond to Granny's challenge? If so, fill in the blanks below with your name, praying as you do for Jesus to make Himself real to you.

I, _____, *choose* this day to believe what I read. I,_____ *choose* this day to take what I've learned about Jesus and let it sink in. I, _____ *choose* this day to believe Jesus understands my pain, is able and willing to help me process my pain caused by rejection, and give me victory over my anger and rage.

I, _____, **choose this day to believe**.   Date: _____

Read Isaiah 53:2-3 from the Life recovery Bible. It is talking about Jesus:

My servant grew up in the Lord's presence like a tender green shoot, like a root in dry round. There was nothing beautiful or majestic about his appearance, nothing to attract us to him. He was despised and rejected—a man of sorrows, acquainted with deepest grief. We turned our backs on him and looked the other way. He was despised, and we did not care.

What does Isaiah 53:2-3 tell you about Jesus?

_____
_____
_____

Now that we have been given the chance to believe that we are never alone in our pain, *and Jesus understands rejection,* let's pray…

"Lord Jesus…We come before You asking You to help us. We have walked through life holding on to pain and sorrow, and because of this, we have developed anger and rage that has caused us to erupt

like a volcano without warning. We realize we are powerless to overcome this in and of ourselves. We come to You now asking You to intervene and to heal us. Set us free, Lord Jesus, from this pain as we realize You understand how we feel. We repent of our reactions to the pain caused by rejection and ask You to teach us how to walk in victory. As we move on in this study, we want to be honest with ourselves and You, and believe You are our ultimate Healer. We expect to overcome anger and rage caused by rejection in Your Mighty Name as we believe Your word! <u>We expect to become life-giving forces instead of deadly volcanoes</u>. Amen"

Before we continue, I'd like to give you an opportunity to write a letter or a prayer to Jesus, thanking Him for understanding where you are coming from:

_____

_____

_____

_____

_____

_____

_____

_____

_____

_____

I want to encourage you to believe that your life can and will change; that you can and will become a life-giving force instead of a deadly volcano because:

<u>**You**</u> have <u>**chosen**</u> to believe:

1. You are not alone.
2. Jesus understands.
3. Jesus cares.
4. Jesus wants to help you.
5. You can and will have victory over anger and rage.
6. Your life can and will change.
7. You will become a life-giving force.

Personal notes:

CHAPTER 4

Natural and Spiritual Volcanoes

Now that we've walked through chapters two and three together, *Our Greatest Need and Critical Choices*, it's time to get back to what happened after I stormed out of Mr. T's office, and see what we can learn…

As if things couldn't get worse, it's dark outside and a light mist is falling. The air is damp and chilly, which adds to my ongoing misery. I hate nights like this. I hate drizzle. I hate mist. My thinking is, if it's going to rain, just do it and move on.

I know Ms. Madeline doesn't see well in the dark, so this could be a *very, very* long ride home. I also know that after my outburst in Mr. T's publishing office, she's probably *not* going to allow me to get behind the wheel.

I resolve myself to what lies ahead but I'm *not* happy about it. Ms. Madeline's far behind me as I am pounding the pavement through the parking garage trying to work off some steam before I get to her van. I'm afraid I'll rip the door off when I open it if I don't.

"Alex!" I look behind and can barely see her. She is coming up the last step and I can just see the top of her head. I tore out of that guy's office and left her in the lurch to fend for herself in the dark. Man! Sometimes I can be so *selfish*.

Look… She's at least thirty years older than I am, drives me around in her van because I still don't have wheels of my own, listens to all my griping, loves me anyway… and *this* is how I treat her?

So, in order to redeem my *selfish* self, I stop and wait.

She's running toward me trying to juggle her umbrella and our files. Why's she using that thing in the first place…it's only *mist*…? Oh well, maybe she just got her hair done or something. I gasp as she trips and falls. Our files scatter all over the place and her polka dotted umbrella rolls away. She's still at least fifty feet from me.

"Ms. Madeline!"

I'm in a panic now because I know she has a *bad* hip and this could turn into a really bad trip. As I'm running toward her I have visions of trying to carry her to the van and driving her to the hospital. And man…I'm like…really *not into that* after the week we've had.

By the time I get to her, she's sitting on the floor rocking and laughing her head off. Ms. Madeline has this way about her…she likes to take a bad situation and *laugh* about it. Says laughter is good medicine. I suspect she learned that from Granny.

I reach for her hand to help her up, and we chase our beloved papers all over the parking garage. She is limping and finally takes both shoes off and throws them to the side.

"Stupid heels. Don't know why I thought it necessary to wear *those* things!" Now free from having to wobble on heels she's not used to, Ms. Madeline has joined me in hot pursuit of our *unsuitable material for a very sensitive readership.*

We snatch up the last of our airborne paper and flop down on the curb. A few cars pass with the passengers trying not to stare at us. "Do we look that bad?"

"I don't know, Alex. Wonder if anybody's run over them high heels. Never was one to wear them no how. Just be me. That's what I'll do next time…"

"Yeah… Ms. Madeline. Just be you. And, I'll just be me. That's what we'll do."

With that, I grab her hand and we get up together. "Where's your van?

"C3 West. Over there." She points.

"OK. Let's go. Who's gonna drive?"

"Don't know, Alex. Guess the first one who gets there."

We look at each other and bust out laughing. Ms. Madeline runs for the pitched shoes and heads for the van. I follow her in amazement. Here's this old lady leading the pack, not missing a beat, and I'm chasing after her holding my chest as though I've just run an Olympic relay race. Guess that shows you the difference between choosing to abuse your body or not. And… so much for worrying about her and her bad hip. Must've been the high heels that got her so far behind me earlier…nothin' wrong with her now!

Ms. Madeline opens the driver's door and I lean against the van, my chest heaving. I lower my head trying to catch my breath before uttering the most ridiculous question I've asked in a long time, "You gonna let me drive?"

"Not on your life, my young friend," she says. She throws our files, her beloved umbrella, and the detestable shoes into the back seat.

"Get in," she says. "We've got some serious talking to do."

I obey and climb in. As she fires up the engine, I look out the passenger window and think about my run-in with Mr. T. My blood starts to boil. Ms. Madeline adjusts the rear view mirror, buckles up, and *slowly creeps* out of the parking spot. I sigh.

Yeah, this is going to be one *very, very* long ride home…

"I know you're right, Ms. Madeline. I know everything you said is right. It don't mean I have to *like* it!" I yell, as I slam the front door.

"Alex! Please. You're gonna break the windows if you don't take it easy. You know Granny spent her last dime fixin' this place up for us. She's probably rollin' over in her grave watching you go off like this!"

"Awe…Ms. Madeline. Don't be so *dramatic*! It just ain't fair of you to use Granny like that."

"Alex…I *MEAN* it!"

"Yes, Ms. Madeline."

I march into the small kitchen where Granny used to fix me biscuits 'n gravy when I was a wild child. I stop and grin as I remember the time she caught me and my buddies trying to sneak in after an all-nighter.

She lined us up in this very room, calmly took our three jugs of moonshine, and slowly poured them down the drain. You should have seen her. She was like a drill sergeant determined to set us straight. We were sick over the loss of our precious brew.

There'd been many a morning she'd stand at the old stove cooking me up some biscuits 'n gravy knowing I was hung over to beat the band. She never said much until I'd get up from the table and she'd whisper, "Alex…one of these days the Good Old Lord's gonna get you and you'll never be the same."

I smile. A tear falls from the corner of my eye as I remember her hugs, her tough love, and her determination to see my life change. I don't know where I'd be now if it weren't for Granny, 'cept rottin' in some penitentiary, I'm sure.

Ms. Madeline retires to her side of the house, and I decide the best thing for me to do is build a fire and get into Granny's letters. I need her help now as never before. I am on the brink of messing up and I know she can stop me, even from the grave. It's been her letters, along with my Bible, that have kept me from getting locked up again.

> So, here I am telling you my story because God still has a plan for me even though it looks *NOTHING* like the plan I had…

I thought things would be different when I got out. I had this unrealistic fairy tale plan going on while I was in prison. I had everything mapped out. I had all the steps figured out. I would get a job. I would buy me some wheels. I would get me a place to live. I would make new, good friends and find me a church…

When I heard the words I waited for years to hear, "*Husdon… Pack it up!*" I had no idea what I was in for when I got out. Nothing happened the way I imagined. There were no jobs. Without a job, you can't get wheels. Without wheels, you can't get to work. Without wheels or a job, you can't get your own place. My fantasyland plans went up in smoke within a month.

I'm not complaining, I'm just telling you the gut-honest truth. It's tough out here when you're a felon…*BUT…then again…GOD.* Granny taught me to say and believe…*BUT GOD.* So, here I am telling you my story because God still has a plan for me even though it looks *NOTHING* like the plan I had…

Sorry, I'm getting off track here. Back to my situation with the publishers, my anger, and Ms. Madeline's insistence that I get control of it. What to do next?

Well, I figure it this way. If I don't get control of this anger and figure out what triggers it, I have a very good chance of blowing it, and ending up right back where I came from…*locked up*. That's definitely *NOT* part of my plan or God's.

Now that I've cooled down, and Ms. Madeline's retired for the night, I'm going to build me a fire and grab some of Granny's letters and my *County* Bible. *I admit I need help…and I need it now.*

I've filed all of Granny's letters in boxes according to the subject matter. Every letter has Bible verses, teaching, and inspiration that go along with whatever issue I was dealing with while I was *locked up*. I'm sure you won't be surprised to find out most of the letters are filed under *A* for *ANGER*.

ANGER…the big A word. What to do with it? How to control it? What causes it?

What do *YOU* think? What do *YOU* think about the big *A* word???

_____

_____

_____

_____

I find some kindling wood and paper and begin to prepare the *atmosphere*. It's all about *atmosphere* sometimes. Now, I know if you are locked up, you don't have much to say about your *atmosphere*. You can't just go and build a fire any time you want to. But, take it from me, there are certain things you *can* control where you are. You can **choose** to do productive things rather than just *doing time*.

I figured that out way too late in life. I believe I wouldn't have spent so many years locked up had I found a better way of doing my time rather than just *doing time*. I could have signed up for education classes and learned something. I could have put down the cards and picked up my Bible. I could have written more to *Granny* instead of trying to get sexual pen-pal relationships going with people I didn't know. I could have walked away from the TV and went to Bible Study. I could have prayed more and stayed more in tune with God and His purposes. Simply put, *I could have used doing time to better myself instead of wasting it.*

Before we move on, I'd like to give you an opportunity to do just that…**choose** to *do productive things* rather than just *doing your time*. Make a list of the things you are spending too much time on that really aren't doing anything but wasting time. Then…list the things you feel you should spend more time doing. Make it a point to daily monitor the things you are doing and **make good choices**.

Things I should spend less time doing:

_____
_____
_____
_____
_____
_____
_____

Things I should spend more time doing:

_____
_____
_____
_____
_____
_____
_____

Sorry about that little *rabbit trail*, but I believe it was important. Granny used to call her rabbit trails *spontaneous wisdom* and I believe she was right. Sometimes you just gotta insert something that seems way out in left field to make a point. Every one of Granny's *rabbit trails* proved to be just what she called them…*spontaneous wisdom*.

OK... So let's get back to this anger issue and see what Granny has to say.

I open the first letter and remember well why Granny had written it. Flashbacks of the incident roll on in my mind like a bad movie. The scene, of course, is *The County* and *once again* old Alex is *out of control*. I remember it as if it were yesterday...

I had been in the hole because I went off on some inmate in my block. There was a picture floating around; a very suggestive picture of my little sister, and it found its way to me. All sense of reality left and in a split second I was going for the throat. With no thought of consequences for my actions, I jumped up and attacked. I couldn't have cared less about rules and regulations. *Anger erupted, quickly turning into rage.* Rage, as if a power of its own, took control of my body, mind, and soul. I heard officers come in shouting and threatening to use mace, but I was beyond reason. I felt the cuffs pinch and I fell as the mace hit, but I was in another world. I had entered the world of *murderous intention*.

As I sat in the hole for days with nothing but my thoughts, I wondered at the speed in which my emotions flew. How could I leave reality so quick? How could I snap like that without warning? One minute, I was playing cards, and the biggest concern of the day was which card to lay down. The next minute I am shackled heading for the hole, screaming in pain from mace, and a bunch of time was being added to my sentence. How did all that happen in a split second?

What is this <u>volcanic power</u> that has the ability to take over my entire being, rendering me incapable of rational behavior?

Granny's response:

Dear Alex,

Here we are again…*discussing another one of your trips to the hole.* By the sound of your last letter, I believe you're at the breaking point, and have actually scared yourself into looking for help. Thank God everyone involved is still alive, we aren't looking at more serious charges, and all you got was another trip to the hole and some more time to do.

I've known you all your life, Alex. I *know* inside that *erupting volcano* there's someone who's been wounded but doesn't know how to process the pain. There's so much good inside of you, Alex. It's just buried underneath piles and piles of *rejection*.

As I'm sure you remember, night after night I sat with you as you waited for your Mamma and Daddy's Eldorado to turn the corner. But after you realized they were never coming back, you gave up and retaliated. Your *pain* turned into *anger* and then into *rage*. I'm not blind, Alex. You thought you were hiding stuff from me, but I was very much in tune to what was going on. I helplessly watched as you spiraled downhill into the world of drugs, booze, sex, and crime. It broke my heart to watch you cover up your pain with everything imaginable, but I was power-less to stop you.

Things went crazy in your mind, Alex, when your life was suddenly turned upside down. You were way too young to understand what was happening. I don't think you ever got over that, *and the pain's been buried so deep you don't even realize it's still there.*

It's like a bad seed waiting to grow into something horrible every time it's watered. When you experience *rejection of any kind*, it *triggers* that bad seed and waters it. The *seed of rejection* sucks up the water and starts to grow. It takes hold of you and turns you into someone *you* don't even recognize.

Pretty soon I'm getting a call from the *County* or some other place telling me to post bond or that you're *locked up*. You want to know what I think? I think it's God's way of keeping you safe until you receive healing and come to your senses.

Why this continuous cycle in your life? Like I've told you before, it's not necessarily what is going on in the present that causes you to *go off* and act crazy, but it's those pent up emotions, or bad seeds, *that have not found their healing.*

I understand why you were *angry* because of that picture, but Alex, you've got to learn to process anger Jesus' way. **You'll never be able to do that until you admit you have a problem and are willing to do what it takes to overcome it.**

Your little sister was one constant in your life, but since her death, you haven't been rational when it comes to *anything* associated with her. In reality, you're experiencing *rejection* from her because she died and it comes out in *rage* every time something triggers it. Simply put, she died…she left you…you feel rejected… and, you *respond* to the *rejection* with *anger* or *rage*. I suspect deep down you were *angry* with her because she wasn't here to defend herself, and your emotions got the better of you.

Rejection is a deep-rooted spirit that forms early in our lives. It has many masks like anger, rage, hate, frustration, confusion, resentment, and mistrust, to name a few. Rarely does it give its victims time to diffuse their responses to it. It is a *hidden spirit* that comes to steal, kill, and destroy anything in its path.

I was reading an article about volcanoes during an adult educational class I was taking while you were *locked up*, back in '09. (I think it was the time you smashed your car into that judge's house. By the way…what *were* you thinkin'?)

Anyhow, I can't believe how a scientific article on a mound of dirt could describe a human being's response to the *spirit of rejection* so perfectly. It had *you* written all through it. I thought… *that's my Alex…a walking, breathing, active volcano waiting to erupt*!

You were insane, Alex. I remember coming to get you out on bond before your trial and you were spittin' nails…and…*the language*…Alex! I had a mind to put you out of the car for your disrespect, but I was afraid you'd go back to the detention center acting crazy like you do, and get yourself *locked up* for good.

You asked me in your last letter what you need to do. I have enclosed a worksheet I wrote for a group study we were doing on the *spirit of rejection*. I believe most of your problems stem from being controlled by this spirit.

I love you so much, Alex, but you will never realize it until this spirit is dealt with. You are a gifted writer, musician, and teacher, but all these gifts are buried along with your pain. I've seen and heard what you are capable of when you aren't out there running around acting crazy. I've seen and heard what God's put in you. With God, you have the power to overcome this, Alex. I believe it with all that's in me, but…

You've got to believe it!

Take your time with this worksheet and expect God to do something big in your life, Alex. *He can take that volcano of destruction you've been controlled by since you were a child, and transform it into a powerful life-giving force to help others.*

You asked me what you need to do. Well, my dear Alex, this is it. *Be willing to* **give your pain to Jesus**, *and* **believe** *He can do what I said He can.*

Write me and let me know how you are doing.

As always…all my Love,
Granny

I pick up Granny's worksheet and settle in to read…

EXPOSING THE VOLCANO'S CORE
THE SPIRIT OF REJECTION
BY GRANNY G.

To understand the *spirit of rejection* and its ability to temporarily render us powerless over our actions and reactions, we must understand the basics of a volcano. There are three stages a volcano may be in. They are the active stage, the dormant stage, or the extinct stage.

The *active stage* is where the volcano *is erupting* or *soon* to *erupt*. The *dormant stage* is where it is *sleeping* and *inactive*, but can be expected to *wake up* and *erupt* in the future. The *extinct stage* is where it is *not active*, nor is it expected to be active or erupt in the future.

Next, let's look at the definitions of *erupt* and *pent up*:

One of the definitions from Webster's Dictionary of *erupt* is: *to force out or release suddenly and often violently something (as lava or steam) that is pent up.*

The definition of *pent up* is: *confined/crowded*

Write the three stages of a *volcano* and define them:

1._____ Definition_____
2._____ Definition_____
3._____ Definition_____

Write out one of Webster's Dictionary's definitions of erupt:

_____

What does pent up mean?

_____

Next, let's take a look at some basic facts about what causes a volcano to *erupt*:

There are 4 basic elements that contribute to the eruption of a volcano:

1. Heat

2. Rock

3. Gasses

4. Pressure

Alone or separate, these four elements are harmless. But, given the right environment, together they become a deadly explosive that causes death and destruction to everything and everyone in its path.

The center of the earth is very hot. It is so hot it can melt solid rock. This melted rock is called *magma* and collects into blobs. Because the blobs are lighter than the surrounding rock, they begin to move toward the earth's surface.

As these blobs rise, the rock around them melts and a *magma chamber* is created. This *magma chamber* becomes a *reservoir* that *holds everything* that will eventually *erupt* from the *volcano*.

Pressure builds as the *magma chamber* fills with the gas-filled *magma* and this *weakens* or *causes fractures* in the surrounding rock. *Escalating pressure* inside the magma chamber eventually drives the magma upward resulting in an eruption through the earth's surface.

This is my understanding of the *hidden dynamics* of a natural volcano's *eruption*. I believe God wants to use it to help us understand our own explosive behavior…

Complete the following sentences from what we've learned so far about a *natural volcano*. You can refer back to the previous paragraphs to find the answers.

The center of the earth is very _____.
The center of the earth is so hot it can_____.
Magma is_____.
Magma collects into _____and_____.
A magma chamber is_____.
Pressure inside the magma chamber_____
and causes_____.

We have just spent a few minutes together learning about *natural volcanoes*. This is what we will call our *natural understanding*. There are *natural facts* we have read and believed which brings us to *natural conclusions* about *natural volcanoes*.

In your own words, explain how a *natural volcano* in the *active* state erupts:

_____

_____

To sum up what we've learned:

natural volcanoes erupt when *natural heat, natural gasses,* and *natural pressure* are *combined under ideal conditions*. This is our *natural understanding of natural volcanoes*.

Next, we will expose the *hidden process* that causes us to *erupt* in *anger* or *rage* when *the spirit of rejection* has been *triggered*. We will call this our *spiritual understanding* of *spiritual volcanoes*. We will uncover *spiritual facts* about the *spirit of rejection* and *come to understand spiritual truths about spiritual volcanoes…our hearts.*

The goal of this spiritual understanding is to expose and conquer this deadly, silent beast...the spirit of rejection.

Read and write the following statement and verses again:

The *heart* is the *center of our being* from which all our actions find their root.

Guard your heart above all else, for it determines the course of your life. Prov. 4:23 (Life Recovery Bible)

As a face is reflected in water, so the heart reflects the real person. Prov. 27:19 (Life Recovery Bible)

Just as a *natural volcano* has hidden elements deep beneath the surface that can cause it to become active and erupt, so do we. Our hearts, *the center of our being*, have been *exposed* to the *spirit of rejection* continually throughout our lives. It is a fact of life...people hurt people. Whether or not they intend to, people hurt us and we get offended.

Let's take a minute to examine the definition of *rejection*. In simple terms, it means to refuse to accept, refuse to hear, refuse to receive, to cast off, to throw back, to spew out (as in vomit.) This is the *act* of *being rejected*.

In addition to the *act* of *being rejected*, we have a term that *defines* a person. This term is *a reject*. According to Webster's Dictionary, this is a person who is someone who is *not wanted, unsatisfactory*, or someone who is *not fulfilling standard requirements*. The words *rejection* and *reject* are to be understood as *outside sources of rejection* for our study.

Let me explain...

During the course of our lives, we experience *rejection from others*. This *rejection* may have come to us in the form of being put up for adoption, through divorce, being fired from a job, being kicked out of school, mental, physical, or sexual abuse, just to name a few.

These are *outside sources* of rejection that *come upon us* through the *actions of others* making us feel *unwanted, unsatisfactory, or sub-standard.*

Take a minute to jot down some things you think may have caused you to experience an *outside source of rejection* due to the *actions of others*...

_____

_____

_____

_____

_____

_____

Next, describe how you feel as you re-visit the event(s) you just wrote about:

_____

_____

_____

_____

If we do not process this *outside source* of *rejection* Jesus' way, it will *find entrance* into the *core of our being* and become a foundation upon which *a spiritual volcano may be built.*

This is how the *spirit of rejection* operates *from the outside*:

1. It *attaches itself* to our outside source of rejection searching for a place to hide and take over.

2. It *finds entrance* into *our hearts* through *cracks* where *unresolved* and *unhealed* wounds are *held captive by unforgiveness.*

3. Once it finds an *unresolved* or *unhealed* wound, the *spirit of rejection attaches itself to it with our unforgiveness* being the *cement* that *holds it in place.*

4. ***Now, the spirit of rejection has a foundation…a place from which to operate.***

5. As the new *outside source of rejection* is *cemented* to our *unresolved or unhealed wound* by our *unforgiveness,* the *spirit of rejection* gains strength and *pressure builds.*

6. It lies in wait until another *outside source of rejection* comes our way.

7. Then, it begins the process all over again. It attaches the new *outside source of rejection* to our existing *unresolved* or *unhealed wounds* that are cemented together by *unforgiveness,* and *gains even more strength.*

Each time we experience a *new source of rejection* and are *unable to process it* God's way *through forgiveness,* we give the *spirit of rejection* more *power to control us.*

We must process these experiences Jesus' way or we will become a walking, breathing, active volcano ready to erupt.

Take a minute to re-read what we've learned about the *spirit of rejection* and how it operates *from the outside*. On the following lines, describe a situation where you believe this was or is happening in your life.

_____

_____

_____

_____

_____

Just like a *natural volcano* forms *natural magma* that collects into *blobs*, our hearts produce *spiritual magma* or *spiritual blobs* each time we do not process hurt or offenses Jesus' way.

As *we ignore* our core's (heart's) condition, more *hot blobs* form each time we experience hurt or offense. Just as in the *natural volcano*, our *spiritual volcano* (our hearts) produce a *hot blob chamber* as the *blobs* of *unresolved hurts* and *offenses* collect together and begin to *rise to the surface*.

As these *spiritual blobs* rise, they *heat* the walls of our heart and *pressure builds* in the chamber. As we learned earlier, in a *natural volcano*, this pressure *weakens* and *causes fractures* in the surrounding rock.

It is the same with our hearts. As our *spiritual blobs* of *hurt* and *offense* rise to the surface, our *hearts weaken and break*. Just think of the words we've all heard before…*a broken heart*. It is at this point where we find ourselves unable to control the outcome.

We have become the *spiritual volcano* ready to *erupt* in *anger* or *rage*. The *hot blobs* of *unresolved hurts* and *offenses* have taken over the heart's chamber and have *collected together* causing *escalated pressure*. When the chamber can no longer hold the pressure, we become the *spiritual volcano erupting and out of control*.

ANGER AND RAGE CAN BE THE OUTSIDE EVIDENCE OF THE INTERNAL CONTROL OF THE SPIRIT OF REJECTION IN OUR LIVES.

Let's review what the Bible says about *our heart*. Read and write the following verses. Consider the condition of *your heart* as it relates to what we've learned about the *spirit of rejection*.

Guard your heart above all else, for it determines the course of your life. Prov. 4:23 (Life Recovery Bible)

As a face is reflected in water, so the heart reflects the real person. Prov. 27:19 (Life Recovery Bible)

If your heart was reflected in water as the above verse indicates, what would you see?

I would see: _____

If we suspected there was something seriously wrong with our heart, we would most likely make an appointment with a heart specialist. He or she would perform some tests in order to make a proper diagnosis of our heart's condition.

We may enter his or her office with *symptoms* such as shortness of breath or chest pains, but the *symptoms* are just that, *symptoms*. The **root cause** of the shortness of breath or chest pains lies in the *condition of the heart*. Until a specialist performs the correct tests, the exact causes are *hidden*.

Likewise, anger can be a *symptom* of an *emotionally broken heart* due to the operation of the *spirit of rejection* in our lives. There can be many **root causes** for *anger*, and just like our physical heart, our emotional heart *needs testing* in order to *correctly diagnose* the **root cause**. We can then determine the best course of action in prescribing treatment.

Let's do a short test together. Place a check mark beside every statement that describes you. I have added blank lines so you can add anything I might have missed.

I get angry:

_____ when I am afraid.
_____ when I have been offended.
_____ when I have been lied to.
_____ when I have been lied about.
_____ when my feelings have been hurt.
_____ when I have been overlooked.
_____ when I feel rejected.
_____ when I am not included.

_____ when things don't go my way.
_____ when I am tired.
_____ when people don't do what they said they would do.
_____ when I am disrespected.
_____ when people hurt someone I love.
_____ when I am ignored.
_____ when what I say doesn't seem important.
_____ when people look down on me.
_____ when I feel out of control of situations.
_____ when I feel unloved.

_____ _____

_____ _____

_____ _____

_____ _____

The list above is not by any means all-inclusive, but it shows us evidence of the *spirit of rejection's* control over us. Remember the definition of *rejection*? It is being not accepted, not listened to, not received, to be cast away, not wanted, unsatisfactory, or not fulfilling standard requirements. Every statement that you checked in the *heart test* above falls into one or more of the categories of *rejection*. Take a minute to examine the places you checked and let's ask Jesus to help you see where you are in the *heart test*.

Dear Jesus:

"I've been *struggling* with *anger* and *need Your help* to overcome it. I realize everything I have tried to do in the past is not working and I'm tired of living life not knowing when I'm going to blow up. My reactions to life's situations have caused me and those I love much pain and sorrow. I am either in my own prison of self-destruction, or in an actual prison with an institution's address as my home. I'm coming to You as humbly as I know how asking for Your help. As I review the things I checked on the heart test I just took, I'm asking You to *reveal to me* the *root causes* of my *anger*.

I want to work through these issues *Your way*. I know *Your way* is the *only way* I will be *set free* to *live the life* You died to give me.

I love You, Jesus, and thank You for listening to my prayer. I know You want to set me free more than I want to be set free. Thank You for helping me overcome this *poisonous anger* that's controlled me all my life."

Your son/daughter_____Date:_____

Go back and review your heart's test. Journal your thoughts below:

I can see where the *spirit of rejection* has taken control of me because:

_____
_____
_____
_____
_____

I feel I need *healing* and *deliverance* from the *spirit of rejection* because:

_____
_____
_____
_____
_____

Personal notes:

_____
_____
_____
_____
_____
_____
_____
_____
_____
_____
_____
_____
_____

CHAPTER 5

Destroying Destructive Vows

I put Granny's worksheet down, and stare into the fire that is, by now, going full force. I'm amazed at how Granny could always get to the bottom of things with me. She had this uncanny way about her. She was able to see through the walls of protection I built around myself over the years, and tried her best to knock them down. She used tough love, soft love, and all kinds of love in between.

But…I was *unwilling to receive* any of it. My mom split after my dad died and I never saw her again. I vowed I'd never let anyone hurt me like that again.

That *vow* became part of my identity and *ruled my reactions to people*. I saw people through the *distorted lenses* of that *vow*, inwardly threw my hands up in the air and said, *no further dude… you're not getting any closer*!

As I stare into this warm, crackling fire, Jesus is helping me realize I didn't even know I had made that *vow*. Flashbacks of events in my life are running through my mind. *Every time* I sensed *any kind* of *rejection* (whether it was real or not)…*BAM*…inconsiderate, uncaring, angry Alex showed up from nowhere.

My reactions were totally out of control and I see that now. I am beginning to understand what was going on. *In order to keep people at a distance so I would not have to experience rejection of any kind, I got angry and blew up at them.*

In some sort of twisted way, this vow I made was ruling my life, and making me think I was protecting myself. Jesus is helping me see it was *all a lie*. The *vow* was *not protecting me*, it was *IMPRISONING me*.

My *anger* and *rage* came in many forms, some of which caused me to get *locked up* more times than I care to admit. I had been *lied to* by the *spirit of rejection*.

I fell victim to its *lie* which taught me to *build walls using anger* in order to protect *myself* from *rejection*!!! What a crock!

The very thing I was trying to protect myself from was using me against myself!!!

I've been *locked up* my whole life! If I wasn't in some institution *doing time*, I was *locked up* emotionally and spiritually. I could not retain any healthy relationship, whether it be with people or with God!

How about you, friend? Are you connecting with any of this? I have an idea you probably are. We've all been beat up by life in one way or another and *made destructive vows* without even knowing it!

Before we get back to my story, I want to give you a chance *to expose* some of the *destructive vows* you've made. Then, we are going to ask Jesus to help you deal with them.

After reading my story, did some *vows* <u>you</u> have made come to mind? Write about them here: (use extra paper if there is not enough space here…get 'em all!)

_____

_____

Do you see these vows in operation in your life? If so…how?

_____

_____

When we speak a *vow* over our lives, we actually *create the atmosphere* for that *vow to operate*. We briefly talked about *creating atmosphere* earlier. This is one type of atmosphere we *can have control over* no matter where we are.

A *vow* is saying *I will* or *I will not*. Our words have power.

Consider Proverbs 18:21:
Death and life are in the power of the tongue, and those who love it will eat its fruit.

In other words, what we say, we will experience. We've all heard this…you'll be sorry, you're gonna eat your words. *Death* or *life…which <u>words</u> will <u>you</u>* **choose?**

If you have made *vows* like I have, and want to *renounce* them (make them incapable of controlling you any longer)…let's talk to Jesus about it…

Dear Jesus,

"I realize now that I have made *destructive vows* in my life because I have been hurt and wounded by others. I want to *renounce* these *vows* and render them *incapable* of controlling me any longer.

These are the *destructive vows* I've made in order to protect myself. I realize they have caused me to live in a self-made prison and I want to be set free…"

I vowed that I (would/would never) _____

_____

_____

_____

I speak to the *vow(s)* and say: (Speak separately for each vow you listed.)

"I recognize you for what you are…*darkness controlling my life*, my relationships with others, and my relationship with God. I renounce the vow of_____

_____

and sever any attachment I have to you in Jesus' name. I consider every word I spoke in *this vow* null and void. In your place I <u>choose</u> to fill my life with God's promises of light and life. You have no authority over me because I am a child of God and Jesus has bought me with His blood. This is settled in heaven and on earth, and, from this moment forward, **I am no longer under your control**."

I speak to the *spirit of rejection* and say…

"Be gone in Jesus' name. You have no authority to operate in my life because these *vows* I made are like bad checks that have no value. *You no longer have the right to control me.* I am wise to the way you operate, and if you try to sneak up on me unaware, ***I will recognize you and throw you out***…In Jesus' name!"

I speak to Jesus and say…

"I *choose* to *speak Your Word* instead of *deadly vows* into my life. I *choose* to combat the *spirit of rejection* with *Your promises*. I *choose* to believe I am being set free. Thank You, Jesus for setting me free…"

Every time you recognize another deadly vow you have made, come back to this exercise and exorcize it and the spirit of rejection from your life!

I lift my head and smile as I look at Granny's picture on the mantle. The picture was taken about a week after a stray puppy hobbled onto our property. She's gazing at the puppy with warm tenderness as she holds it close to her heart. She named the puppy Elsie, in honor of my sister, who died way too young after leaving Carlucci's dope house a while back. But…we won't get into that now…

Anyhow, when Elsie showed up, she was dragging one of her hind legs, barely able to walk. We figured she got it caught in a barbed wire fence somewhere because blood oozed out of it. Her hair was matted and full of ticks. She had a collar but no identification tag. The collar was so tight it rubbed a sore in her neck. We thought someone just dropped her out on the road behind the woods. She was skin and bones, and didn't look like she'd live for more than a few days.

Granny said, "Alex…we'll feed her, give her some water, and if she dies, at least she won't die hungry and thirsty." Well, Granny's love won again. Elsie lives a pampered, happy life to this day.

I feel a warm tear slowly creep down my cheek as I realize I am like the wounded puppy in the picture. When I came to stay at Granny's, I had no home, no parents, and felt all alone in the world. I wasn't physically wounded, but *I was emotionally and spiritually crippled.*

She took me in, raised me, loved me, and did her best to guide me. Her love was genuine. But, *unlike Elsie,* I was *unable to receive* her love because of what had happened to me.

Because I was being controlled by the spirit of rejection, I could not receive Granny's love.
Even though I didn't realize it, I kept her at a safe distance *in my heart,* because *deep down,* I didn't trust her. I was afraid if I let her in, she would leave me just like my parents did.

The vow I made years ago continuously strained my relationship with Granny and ruined every other one. In all my craziness, I've come to realize that…

Most of what I struggle with is rooted in the fear of being rejected by others.

One day Granny was driving me home from *The County*. It was the third time she had to bail me out. "Alex," she said, "I don't understand why you need to go around and do all this crazy stuff. What are you running from? What are you trying to prove? What are you searching for?

I'll tell you what I think…I think you're searching for love…*for true love.* And, you're searching in all the wrong places. I hear you sneak in, tripping all over the place, mumbling about somebody stealing your car keys or your date, or some other incoherent babble. It's a real shame to hear your beautiful voice being used to cuss, rant and rave, and mumble as you stumble to your room.

What you haven't figured out yet, is that I stay up every night to make sure you make it home in one piece. I hear you cry yourself to sleep in frustration as you beat your fists into your pillow. You're all mixed up, Alex, because you try to hide behind booze, sex, and drugs.

All this running around and carrying on has given you a false identity, and covered up the real you. <u>I don't think you even know who you are anymore</u>.

Why don't you stop running long enough to let Jesus love you and show you who you *really are*? You're never going to be satisfied in life until you know how much you are loved. That's what you're looking for…you're looking for true love. But, because of stuff that's happened to you, *you don't believe it really exists.*

That's why you're running…that's why you're hiding. I'm going to tell you something, Alex. People are not perfect. They hurt us, and sometimes it's not even intentional. But at any rate, we cannot rely on people to satisfy our need for true love. Only Jesus can do that. Only He can love us totally, unconditionally, and perfectly.

Why don't you stop running long enough to let Jesus love you and show you who you *really are*?

You are going to run yourself ragged, abusing your body with drugs, alcohol, and sex until you are used up like an old Raggedy Ann doll, and you still won't be satisfied. You'll still be the empty, angry, hurt Alex who's searching for true love.

Why don't you give it up, Alex? Why don't you run to the One Who has the answers for you? He's waiting for you…you know."

I remember this conversation as if it happened yesterday. Her car stunk to high heaven with orange citrus air freshener. It was her favorite. It was so strong I had to roll my window down and gasp for air.

"Alex, she said, "Roll that window back up, I just got my hair done." "Awe…now Granny…you know you're beautiful when you fuss?" I rolled it up half way.

"ALEX!"

"Yes 'um?" She gave me that *Granny look* and I took a deep breath and rolled it the whole way up. "OK, Granny. If'n I'm passed out when we get home, you can be sure it weren't moonshine this time!" We both laughed and I ducked as she reached over and tried to mess with my hair. It was only a few blocks and we would be home.

"How's Elsie doin'?"

"Fine…wild as ever. She'll be on the porch waitin' for us."

I smile as I remember seeing Elsie for the first time in 10 months. That's how long I was *locked up* that time. She was sitting on the front porch just like Granny said. Her tail was going a hundred miles an hour; and she ran like lightning down the steps when she saw me.

I remember thinking…*man's best friend…how true…dogs don't ever give you any lip, always make you feel special, and they're faithful to the end.* I opened the car door and Elsie jumped up on me. We ended up rolling all over the front yard together and only stopped when I heard, "Alex, y'all stop now…you're getting too close to my flower beds!"

Granny and I sat on the porch that evening with Elsie at our feet, watching the sun set. "Alex," she said as I was brushing Elsie's coat. "Jesus is a lot like Elsie. He's man's best friend. He's always there for us when we decide to come back home. He's always happy to see us and shows us in His own special way. He loves our company, and wants to be with us all the time…

You are a lot like Elsie was. Elsie came to us wounded and bleeding. She looked like she was going to die any minute. But, Elsie responded to love and care and her wounds began to heal. She got stronger every day as she ate and drank."

Alex, *I believe she's alive today because she responded to our kindness and care.*

Jesus has provided everything you need, Alex, to live and not die. He has given you Himself. He is the food and water you need. He has taken all your cares upon Himself and offers you His healing. Like Elsie, you need to respond to His food and water, to His kindness and care. It is a choice, Alex. ***You must choose***.

You can choose to run around and hide from yourself and everyone else and eventually die a wounded, angry, person. Or, you can, like Elsie, choose to respond to everything Jesus has provided and live… ***The choice is up to you***."

When Elsie came to us, she had some serious problems. On the lines provided, list some of these problems:

_____

_____

What was Granny's reaction to Elsie's serious problems?

_____

What was Elsie's reaction to Granny's kindness and care?

_____

What was Elsie's part in her ability to live and not die?

_____

What were some of my serious problems when I went to live at Granny's?

_____

_____

How did Granny react to my serious problems?

_____

_____

How did I react to Granny's kindness and care?

_____

_____

Explain the difference between my reactions to Granny's kindness and care and Elsie's, and how it affected our lives:

_____

_____

_____

Do you relate more to my reactions to Granny's kindness and care or to Elsie's? Explain your answer using something from your own life:

_____

_____

_____

What was Granny trying to help me understand about Jesus?

_____

_____

_____

Read the following verses and write them out on the lines provided. (They are the words of Jesus.) Then, in your own words, explain what they mean to you:

"I am the living bread which came down from heaven. If anyone eats of this bread, he will live forever; and the bread that I shall give is My flesh, which I shall give for the life of the world." John 6:51

_____

_____

_____

On the last day, that great day of the feast, Jesus stood and cried out saying, "If anyone thirsts, let him come to Me and drink. He who believes in Me, as the Scripture has said, out of his heart will flow rivers of living water." John 7:37,38

_____

_____

_____
_____
_____
_____
_____
_____
_____

Elsie *received* Granny's kindness and care by *receiving* the food and water she provided. Elsie *lived and did not die* because she ate and drank from what Granny provided her. Elsie lived her *natural life* because *she received* her *natural food and water*.

Do you remember earlier that we talked about *natural volcanoes* and *spiritual volcanoes*? Well, here we are talking about *natural food and water* and *spiritual food and water*.

We can *receive* Jesus' kindness and care by *receiving* the *spiritual food and water* He has provided. It is by *receiving Jesus* and what He has done for us we *receive our spiritual food and water*.

By receiving this spiritual food and water, we will spiritually live and not die.

I want to give you an opportunity to *receive* this *spiritual food and water* before we go any further…

Pray with me or create your own prayer to Jesus. He is waiting!

Dear Jesus,

"I know I am suffering from spiritual mal-nutrition and I recognize my need for Your spiritual food and water. I am wilting like a plant without water, and weak from lack of food. I come to You right now and ask You to fill me with Your bread and water as the verses I just wrote out promise. I thank You, Jesus, that You have heard my prayer and I am being filled to overflowing right now. I ask You to remind me each and every day to pray for a new filling of Your Bread from heaven and Your Living Water."

I love You, Jesus! Your beloved child,_____."

The *destructive vow* I made to never let anyone close enough to hurt me like my parents did caused me to keep everyone at a distance. When they got too close, my sub-conscience took over and made sure the relationship was broken.

In the worst cases, I engaged in physical confrontations which caused me to get *locked up*. The *destructive vow* could always find fault with someone and *triggered* various degrees of *anger* in my *spiritual magma chamber*. Because I was unaware of this *destructive vow*, I was incapable of understanding why I could not control my *anger*.

Please don't continue to live life like I was, in and out of jail and prison because of an *uncontrollable explosive personality*.

Take your time with this *destructive vow* thing. It was a real trip for me when I first realized what was going on. Heavy *stuff*…a lot of it was. But, Jesus is kind, compassionate, caring, and WISE.

He never showed me more than I could handle at one time. He stood by me during the whole process, and never left my side. I could be open and honest about my feelings without being afraid. He held me as I cried, screamed, pounded my fists, and asked Him, "Why?" He brushed my tears, calmed my nerves, and offered me His heart. I trusted Him to help me through, and He did more for me than you could ever imagine.

The only way to freedom is to come to Him with all your *stuff*, trust Him to take you through your own process, and let Him lead the way. I don't know what it will look like for you, because we are all different. What I *do know* is this…He has a perfect plan, and that plan includes *setting you free from your pain*.

Do like I did…*choose* to believe He has come to set you free!

For I know the plans I have for you, says the Lord.
They are plans for good and not for disaster,
to give you a future and a hope.
In those days when you pray, I will listen.
If you look for me wholeheartedly
you will find me.
I will be found by you,
says the Lord…

Jeremiah 29:11-14
Life Recovery Bible

CHAPTER 6

Conquering Flashbacks and Triggers

As I get up to stir the fire, I think about my two best friends who taught me about love…Granny, who's buried in the local cemetery, and Elsie her stray puppy, who's unconditional love never ceases to amaze me.

Elsie watches as I grab Granny's picture from the mantle and gaze into the eyes of the one whose *tough love* loved me to life…

Granny, I hope you're looking down and can see the stuff you've tried to get me to understand is finally starting to click. You know how hot-headed I am, but I want you to know I'm trying to do you proud… and that I love you…

I know I messed up big time in Mr. T's Publishing office by going off at him like that…and poor Ms. Madeline…but Granny…that guy…he…

A loud *pop* comes from the fire and a log falls off the grate and rolls onto the floor in front of my feet. I reach out to grab it with the poker, and, for a second, I think I see Granny's face in the log with that *look* of hers…and I smile.

Yeah…Granny…I know…

I hear her strong voice loud and clear as if she was standin' right here with me…

ALEX…YOU GOTTA FORGIVE…

I put the escaped log back on the fire and turn toward my favorite chair. It used to be Granny's. The cushion is faded and worn… but…oh…so comfortable. I imagine Granny curled up with her pen, paper, and worn out Bible sitting in front of the fire on a cold night. Often, she'd be writing words of wisdom to inspire me in whatever place I was *locked up in* at the time.

I sink in, arranging the cushion to fit the contour of my body. Ms. Madeline is probably sawing logs by now, and Elsie's lying quietly at my feet. Well...not *at* my feet, but *on* them. She loves doing that, and I surely don't mind...she's keepin' the old toes warm on this bitter, cold night. I lean over and stroke her head. She rolls over on her back and waits for a belly rub. I rub her belly with one hand, and grab another one of Granny's letters with the other. This one is filed under "F." It's her worksheet on *forgiveness*.

We both settle in for a nice, quiet night...or so I thought.

I'm just about to open Granny's letter; and Elsie's up in a flash running toward the front window barking like crazy. Ms. Madeline comes out of her room wiping her eyes in half a trance. "What's with Elsie, Alex?"

"Don't know. Suppose I'll have to go out and see...probably nothing...you know how she barks at anything; a fly, a leaf, the wind...Elsie, go lay down." She turns and whimpers as she obeys the command. She flops down, letting me know she's not happy by letting out a big sigh before she curls up beside the ottoman. Her eyes follow me as I grab my coat off the hook and head out the front door.

The minute I reach the front steps, I hear laughter and tires squealing as something flies past my head, crashes through the front window, and lands on the living room floor. Elsie is back at it barking her head off, and Ms. Madeline is crying ... "*Jesus, oh Jesus, oh Precious Jesus!*"

My first instinct is to chase them down and pound them to the ground. Who the h--- are you? What the h--- you doing? No, I'll pound them to the ground *first*... then ask questions.

As I look down the road, reality sinks in and I realize they're long gone. It all happened so fast I didn't get a chance to ID the car or get a license plate. D---it to h---. Nothing left to do but go in and see what's going on.

Ms. Madeline's sitting on the floor just like she was in the parking garage but this time she's not laughing, she's sobbing. She's holding out a broken bottle. To her right on the floor are some newspaper articles and pages from a couple porn magazines. Beside them is a note written in what appears to be blood. She starts rocking and mumbling, "*Jesus, Sweet Jesus,*" as she holds her head in her hands.

Elsie's hiding under the end table. When the bottle flew through the window, the noise must have scared her. Granny told me when she was just a puppy, she took her to a 4th of July celebration in a big field where they were shooting off m80's and m100's. She was terrified. Granny said she hid under the dash of her car back then. Now, when she hears loud noises, she hides under the end table. I look and she is shaking. "It's gonna be ok, Elsie girl. It's gonna be ok." I'm not sure I want to get any closer to the articles and photos. I have no idea what's in them, but instinct tells me it can't be anything good. I am *so angry* now my *heart is racing to its limit.*

I send up what I have come to know as *my life-preserver prayer*. It's simply, *Help, God! I'm fixin' to be in a bad fix if You don't help me…like now!* And, let me tell you, I'm not even saying it out loud. All I can do is *think it*. I don't trust myself to open my mouth…

I know my limitations, and I'm at the boiling point. It isn't helping me one bit that Ms. Madeline has come completely unglued. Miraculously, my prayer is answered. I take a deep breath and walk toward the broken bottle and pile of incriminating evidence.

The calm I experienced was short-lived as I laid eyes on the first newspaper headline…*ERIC HUDSON OF KINGSPORT DRIVE DIES INSTANTLY AFTER SLAMMING HEAD-ON INTO A TREE…*

Look out! Here come the flashbacks!

I slump to the floor with my hands shaking as I grab the paper from Ms. Madeline. I am *so hurt and angry* I can barely breathe…the memories come flooding in…

I'm about 9 years old. People are milling around the living room and nobody will tell me what happened. It's like I'm invisible or something. *Where's my dad! Where's my mom?* Everyone has the same stare.

"Alex, we'll talk later." Granny said. The people walk around all bummed-out looking, but nobody says anything to me. Granny yells at some guys staggering in the front door holding bottles of booze. "Get that stuff out of this house immediately! Hasn't it caused enough grief for this family yet?"

The guests leave without saying a word. That leaves only me, Granny, and a couple of my parent's high school friends. They didn't bring any booze with them; they all got high before they came. Even at nine, I knew. I saw enough of it…

I shake my head to get a grip and read through tears of anger, hurt, and unbelief:

Eric Hudson, 38 of Kingsport Drive died instantly after his car slammed into a tree at the end of Old Ridge Road approximately 3:00 a.m., the Coroner's report states. Undisclosed sources state that Hudson left Rocky's Bar and Grille yelling, "I'm gonna kill the S.O.B. soon as I find him."

Apparently, Hudson was told by one of Rocky's patrons that his wife of 15 years was having an affair with another patron, whose name was not disclosed. Sources report that Hudson's wife was dealing drugs with this unnamed patron and owed him a large sum of money, which she could not pay.

Sources also report Hudson immediately went after his wife, Sarah, who was at the bar with him. As the owner pulled Mrs. Hudson aside to protect her, Tri-County Police were summoned. Hudson fled the scene with Tri-County Sheriff's Department close behind. It is believed that Hudson's car was going 65 miles an hour when he hit the tree. Sarah Hudson is believed to be on the run, and is wanted for questioning.

There it was…in black and white. *What I was never told stared me in the face and pierced my heart with unimaginable pain.* I saw RED!

I reach for more. "Alex…no."

"Ms. Madeline, it's alright. I've got to face this stuff head-on or I'm never going to be free from it. Didn't Granny always say, 'The truth'll set ya free, Alex…the truth is sure to set you free.' Well, I'm going take her up on it. Here it is…the truth right here in black n' white."

I lift my head toward the ceiling and say, "Well, here it is, Granny. The truth…and according to you I'm fixin' ta get set free…" I throw the paper on the table beside my chair and pick up the fireplace poker.

For a minute I think about hunting down whoever did this and make sure they know just who they're messin' with. But, then Granny's voice wins again. *Alex, you gotta forgive…you gotta fogive the whole lot of them…startin' with your mamma and your daddy…you gotta forgive 'em all.*

I respond by putting the poker in its holder and walk out of the room.

"Alex…I had no idea," Ms. Madeline says. I pull up a chair in the kitchen and stare out the window. Granny's vegetable garden is still out there. Well, of course Granny's not here to take care of it, but we still call it Granny's. There's nothing to look at because it's still winter, but it doesn't matter. I wouldn't be able to see anything through the anger and tears anyway.

"Don't feel bad, Ms. Madeline…me and Granny… we never talked about it much. She tried to help me move on with life without my mamma and daddy, and did a right good job. This is just something we didn't talk about.

To tell the truth, I think she thought it best that way. I was a raving maniac every time the subject was brought up and I refused to go to counseling. All I wanted to do was get even…but there wasn't anyone to get even with. You know…the day my mom split…I've never seen her since. And, my old man is buried in the pauper's grave, cause, 'course they didn't have no insurance. Never been to that grave…ever…"

A rush of adrenaline causes me to jump up and pound my fist on the table. "Look here, Ms. Madeline. Look at this stuff. It's not even original…they're all copies! Who on earth copied all this trash, stuffed it into a bottle, and threw it through our window…and *WHY DID THEY DO IT???*"

"Can't answer that, Alex. You got anybody who'd want to get back at you for anything?" She rubs my back trying to calm me. It sort of works.

"Beats me, Ms. Madeline…burned a lot of bridges in my time, you know."

TRIGGERS AND FREEDOM
By Alex Hudson

Life is full of triggers, and the longer we live, the more we have stored in *our hearts*, our *dormant volcanoes*. A trigger is defined in Webster's Dictionary as *something that acts like a mechanical trigger in initiating a process or reaction.*

In more user-friendly terms, let's say a *trigger* is something that *makes us react without our consent.*

For the sake of this study, we will define *trigger* as the *spirit of rejection* buried deep within our *wounded hearts* waiting for *another outside source of rejection* to *find its way in.*

Here's how I see things:

1. I was caught off guard by some truth about my past that was very painful. These truths about my past were *outside sources of rejection.*

2. These *outside sources of rejection* caused the *spirit of rejection* inside me to come alive.

3. The *spirit of rejection ignited memories* and *transported* me back to the place and time as I remembered it.

4. Unresolved hurts and wounds from this part of my past surfaced in anger and the desire for revenge.

That whole process took…what? ***Less than a second!*** We can be going along through life smoothly, and *BAM*, we are knocked down as if someone hit us with a 2x6 on the back of the head.

Looking back on what happened to me when I saw the article about my parents, I see that even in the midst of extreme pain, I could hear God speaking. It may have been through Granny's voice, but it was God speaking. Although the truth I had to face was unbearable, God made sure I was reminded that the truth was going to set me free. (See John 8:32 and 8:36)

I HAD A CHOICE TO MAKE:

1. To allow the truth to destroy me,

or

2. To allow the truth to set me free.

During this extremely painful time, I decided to listen. I decided to explore the possibility that this situation was going to be for my good. I put my trust in God's Word over what I was reading and experiencing.

I opened my *wounded heart* to the One whose promise is to heal the broken-hearted and set the captives free.

Let's review God's Word on this matter…

Write the following verse on the lines provided, and describe in your own words what they mean to you. It is speaking of Jesus:

The Spirit of the Lord God is upon Me, Because the Lord has anointed Me to preach good tidings to the poor; He has sent Me to heal the brokenhearted, To proclaim liberty to the captives, And the opening of the prison to those who are bound. (Isaiah 61: 1)

Verse:

_____

_____

_____

_____

Isaiah 61:1 speaks to me in my situation:

_____

_____

_____

Let's review what God's Word says about truth. Write the following verses out:

Jesus said to him, "I am the way, the truth, and the life…" John 14:6

_____

_____

"And you shall know the truth, and the truth shall make you free." John 8:32

_____

_____

"Therefore, if the Son makes you free, you shall be free indeed." John 8:36

_____

_____

Jesus is the Son.
The Son sets me free.
Jesus is the truth.
The truth sets me free.

IT IS JESUS WHO SETS ME FREE

Write three times: IT IS JESUS WHO SETS ME FREE!!!

_____

_____

_____

Personal notes:

CHAPTER 7
Praying God's Word During Times of Pain and Sorrow

"Ms. Madeline….this is some heavy stuff," I say as I stare into space.

"Alex…I don't know what to say…"

"There is nothing to say Ms. Madeline…"

Elsie curls up beside me as I look though the papers with a sick feeling in my gut. I start picking up pieces of glass. Elsie, my ever present friend in time of need, senses my despair. I lean over to pat her head, silently thanking her for her comforting devotion.

She looks up with sympathetic eyes and licks my hand. You know…there's nothing like the love of an animal. They sense your pain, and are faithful to stick with you to the bitter end.

Anyhow, Ms. Madeline is picking up the rest of the papers. She softly weeps and petitions her greatest friend, Jesus, on my behalf. I suspect He's telling her to not to say much, but just to be here for me.

Most of the mess is picked up and the papers are lying on the table beside my chair. "Didn't know what you wanted me to do with them," she says.

"That's fine, Ms. Madeline." We quickly embrace and stare into the fire.

"I think I'd like to be alone," I say. "You get on to bed. We got a long day tomorrow. Remember, we gotta meet that publisher over on Sixth Street in the morning? And then…the other one down town after lunch?"

"Yeah…I guess…That's if you're up to it."

Ms. Madeline retires to her side of the house and I reach for my pen and journal. Elsie curls up beside me. This is my favorite place to be when things are rough. It is a place of refuge in the storm. Writing has always been a source of comfort and healing for me during the dark days. The warmth of the fire is an added comfort.

As I reach for my pen, I am reminded that God wants us to comfort each other as He comforts us. In the future, I may meet someone who is going through a tough time, and I will be able to help them like God is helping me now.

The Apostle Paul says it like this in 2 Corinthians 1:3-4:

Blessed be the God and Father of our Lord Jesus Christ, the Father of mercies and God of all comfort, who comforts us in all our tribulation that we may be able to comfort those who are in any trouble, with the comfort with which we ourselves are comforted by God.

Paul says we can be there for others when they're hurting because we've experienced God being there for us.

I can think of plenty of people who could use a shoulder to cry on… how 'bout you? No matter where we go, people are hurting. Paul says we can *be there* for others when they're hurting because we've experienced God *being there* for us.

That's why I'm sharing my story with you. Our stories of *rejection* may have different scenes and actors, but the same malicious force directs them…*darkness* and *death*. I want to share what God's taught me through Granny about *rejecting* this dark force, *embracing Jesus*, the Giver of light, and with Him, *embracing life*.

During this intense scene, I know Jesus will meet me where I am and *carry me through* because He's done it before. The Bible tells me that I can come boldly to His throne of grace in my time of need. (See Hebrews 4:16) I do this by writing my thoughts and emotions out, and using His promises in the Bible to speak to Him. I don't hide anything from Him…He knows my heart anyway, so why not?

This is what I do when I *journal*. That's just another name for a dialogue between me and my Heavenly Father. I get gut-level honest with myself and Him. I'm going to write about this evening's events, and I'd like to share my entry with you. I pray my honesty will help you be honest with yourself and God during the dark days in your life…

I like to give them titles and dates to help me remember what was going on…

MY JOURNAL ENTRY
Airborne Bottle of Crap
5/04/13

Abba Father... I have no idea what is going on or why this is happening, but I put my trust in You. I believe You are good, and have my best interests in mind. Your Word says Your ways are higher than my ways, and right now my ways are no ways. I have become numb to protect myself because I don't think I can process one more painful thing. My mind is so full and my heart is so heavy. I have no One but You. You are The Only Constant in my life, and Your mercies never fail. I need Your peace. I need Your rest. Your Word says that when father and mother leave me, You will be there. Your Word says that I am Your beloved child and You will never leave me or forsake me. No matter what things look like now, Your Word is truth, and says I am special in Your eyes. No matter what people say or do, I can always rely on You to love me perfectly.

Your Word says that I can come boldly to Your throne of grace in my time of need because of what Jesus has done for me.

I present this painful situation to You, knowing that You know all things. I present this to You, knowing that before You formed me in my mother's womb, You knew me. You wanted me, so You gave me life. It was You who gave me life, not my mother or my father. They were the vessels You used to give me life. My life is important to You no matter what other people do or say. You have loved me with an everlasting love from before the beginning of time. Your love never fails. It is true, pure, and whole. Your love exceeds any human love. Your love is perfect, and it casts out all my fear.

Whatever is going on in my life is no surprise to You. You knew this was going to happen before time began. You knew this and made provision for me to handle anything that comes my way. Your provision is in Your Son Jesus and what He has done for me. Your provision is in His love for me and His sacrifice on the cross so that I can be whole.

Every bit of painful truth that comes before me is an opportunity to rest in Your care. Every painful experience is an opportunity to experience Your love in a deeper way. Every painful trial is an opportunity to forgive again and be set free from bitterness, anger, and revenge.

I ask You to help me process this thing that happened tonight in a way that I will grow closer to You recognizing that You have everything I need. I ask that I will be stronger and better because of it. I ask You to hold me close to Your heart so I can hear it beating for me. Tender Father, I come to You broken, shattered, and scared...comfort me as I move forward.

Abba Father, be near me as I read these things that flew through our window this evening, and open my eyes to what You would have me see. Teach me through Your Spirit what I need to know to be set free. Remind me of Your Word.

Abba Father, I choose to forgive those who have done this thing as Your Word instructs me to do. I ask You to forgive them because they don't know what they are doing. I ask You to reveal Yourself to them, and help them come to know You and the true peace that only You can give. I ask You to save them, whoever they are, and to bring them into Your Kingdom.

Use this painful time in my life for Your kingdom, that I may help someone else who is hurting...If I could feel Your love right now, I know it would keep me until the pain goes away...

Abba Father, into Your care I commit this pain and myself to You...

Your beloved child...Alex. P.S. A good night's sleep would be appreciated...

Your thoughts on my journal entry:

_____

_____

_____

Is there anything in my journal entry you can relate to?

_____

_____

_____

Now that Elsie's asleep and the fire is dying down, I'm getting ready to call it a night, and man, has it been a night! I lay my pen down and pick up my journal. I want to re-read what I wrote so that when I hit the bed, it is fresh in my mind.

I am choosing to meditate on my journal entry that's full of praying God's Word rather than on what happened.

Every time I write and talk to God, the spirit of heaviness lifts and I feel lighter. Granny taught me *to journal* using *the promises in the Bible*. "There's just something about talking to God in His language that lifts my spirit and brings me peace no matter what's going on." She said.

And, as always…Granny was right.

It strengthens me when I do this because *His word is alive* and brings light into my darkness. It helps me move forward without fear because I am reminding myself that He is by my side, and promises never to leave me in my mess all alone.

I trust you will enjoy this next exercise, and learn how *you too* can *go boldly* to God, and find *comfort* and *strength* by…

Praying God's Word during times of pain and sorrow and writing it down!

I'm going to write out some verses from the Bible that came to mind while I was talking to God about this painful experience I had tonight.

Under the verses, I am going to put some lines. I want to invite you to go back to my journal entry and find the sentence or sentences you think match the verse…then write them on the lines provided. Use extra paper if needed.

Jeremiah 1:5: "Before I formed you in the womb I knew you; Before you were born I sanctified you; I ordained you a prophet to the nations."

_____

_____

_____

Proverbs 3:5-6: "Trust in the Lord with all your heart, And lean not on your own understanding; In all your ways acknowledge Him, And He shall direct your paths."

_____

_____

_____

Isaiah 55:8: "For My thoughts are not your thoughts, Nor are your ways My ways," says the Lord.

_____

_____

_____

_____

John 14:27: "Peace I leave with you. My peace I give to you; not as the world gives do I give to you. Let not your heart be troubled, neither let it be afraid."

_____

_____

_____

Matthew 11:28: "Come to Me, all you who labor and are heavy laden, and I will give you rest."

_____

_____

_____

Hebrews 13:5: ... "I will never leave you nor forsake you."

_____

_____

_____

Psalm 119:160: The entirety of Your word is truth, and every one of Your righteous judgments endures forever.

_____

_____

_____

Hebrews 4:16: Let us therefore come boldly to the throne of grace, that we may obtain mercy and find grace to help in time of need.

_____

_____

_____

Jeremiah 31:3: The Lord has appeared of old to me, saying; "Yes, I have loved you with an everlasting love; Therefore with lovingkindness I have drawn you."

_____

_____

_____

Isaiah 53:5: But He was wounded for our transgressions, He was bruised for our iniquities; The chastisement for our peace was upon Him, And by His stripes we are healed.

James 1: 2-4: My brethren, count it all joy when you fall into various trials, knowing that the testing of your faith produces patience. But let patience have its perfect work, that you may be perfect and complete, lacking nothing.

John 8:32: "And you shall know the truth, and the truth shall make you free."

Ephesians 4:32: And be kind to one another, tenderhearted, forgiving one another, even as God in Christ forgave you.

Colossians 3:13: Bearing with one another, and forgiving one another, if anyone has a complaint against another; even as Christ forgave you, so you also must do.

1 Thessalonians 5:11: Therefore comfort each other and edify one another, just as you also are doing.

2 Corinthians 1:3-4: Blessed be the God and Father of our Lord Jesus Christ, the Father of mercies and God of all comfort, who comforts us in all our tribulation that we may be able to comfort those who are in any trouble, with the comfort with which we ourselves are comforted by God.

_____

_____

_____

The reason I was able to write my thoughts and emotions in my journal, and talk to God in His language, is because I keep reading the Bible, and He reminds me of what I have read.

Jesus tells us how this works in John 14:26:

"But the Helper, the Holy Spirit whom the Father will send in My name, He will teach you all things and bring to your remembrance all things that I said to you."

Write John 14:26 on the lines below:

_____

_____

_____

This is a promise from Jesus Himself. As we read the Bible, we are reading God's word, and Jesus says He will help us remember what we have read.

That is what was happening when I wrote in my journal after the bottle went flying through our front window.

Whenever I am faced with something I don't think I can handle, _I ask God to remind me of His promises._ I write my thoughts and feelings down, and discuss the situation with God.

It keeps the line of communication open as I open my heart to Him at its deepest level where all my pain and suffering reside.

It helps me process what is happening to me without getting bitter, angry, and explosive.

The _inner volcano_ that wants to control me and cause me to go off every time something painful comes my way is **_tamed by declaring God's promises_**.

The volcano is silenced when it hears God's word. It loses its power over me as I continue to write, read, and speak God's promises into my life.

I have *not arrived* by any stretch of the imagination, but I can tell you things are easier to handle when I do it Granny's way…which is God's way.

I receive so much relief, healing, and encouragement every time I *journal* my thoughts and emotions that I want to invite you to *journal* about a painful experience in your life.

Use my journal as a guide. Talk to God about your experience. During this time of writing, ask God to remind you of the promises He has spoken to you through His Word…the Bible. Take your time. This is *one of the greatest weapons* we have *to combat our inner volcanoes*. If you have a Bible handy, get it out and keep it close by. If you have a concordance, that's even better. It will help you locate verses as you think of them.

Before you start, I want to pray with you…

Dear Jesus:

*"Although what I am about to write is very painful and I've never truly processed it Your way, I am asking You to help me face the situation with Your eyes and heart. I am asking You to come and hold me while I write, and help me be **totally honest** about the **whole thing**. I am asking You to help me see things from Your perspective, and take the first steps in allowing You, the Truth, to set me free. I realize now that You are the only One who can help me. I want to start living my life as a life-giving force instead of a deadly volcano. Please help me face this situation head on and process it Your way. Thank You for hearing my prayer and helping me as I write.*

I thank You, Jesus, that Your Word says You will bring to my remembrance everything You have said to me. I thank You, that as I write, You are with me and will help me remember Your promises to me.

I trust You with this deep, emotional trauma, and ask You to heal me and set me free from the spirit of rejection that causes me to lash out in anger and rage.

In Your mighty…powerful…precious name…Amen."

Now, begin to write as if you were talking to your best friend. Write about this painful time and tell God what you are feeling. Use the promises I used in my journal entry and the exercise after it to help you write. Thank God for being with you even if you didn't know He was there. Thank Him for all the promises He has given…

Dear God,

CHAPTER 8

Conquering the Night Season

Elsie follows close behind as I retire to the other end of the house. I've finished washing up, brushing my teeth, and making sure all the towels are where they're supposed to be. If not, Elsie will have me on a chase after she's snatched one. She thinks it's a great game...I think otherwise. Many a night I've had to chase her all over the house because she's real good at getting into places I can't reach. Then she runs off to another...makes for an exhausting end of the day.

Anyhow, tonight I've been alert, and didn't leave anything lying around that she could snatch up. "Elsie girl...time for bed." She scurries over and flops down on her favorite rug. Granny made it years ago, and it lies at the foot of the bed.

Every night she does this spinning around deal before flopping...she spins around three times as fast as she can, then she stops and flops. It's hilarious. You ought to see it. I grin as I reach down to pet her and say goodnight. "Yeah...Elsie girl...you are one hilarious round hound." (I gave her that nickname since she's starting to *fill out* eating too many biscuits...if you know what I mean.)

This used to be Granny's room and Elsie's slept in here since the first night she showed up. Granny said she was an angel sent by God to help her through tough times. No matter how strong Granny tried to pretend to be, Elsie knew better.

Granny was really upset one night...said she didn't feel like talking 'cause no one would understand. She walked out the kitchen door feeling defeated and alone. As she sat on the deck to watch the sunset, a warm body snuggled up against her. It was Elsie...warm, compassionate Elsie. Didn't say a word...and gave no advice. ...Just a warm, friendly, round hound loving Granny and catching her tears on the top of her head.

Yeah, Granny was right. Elsie was an angel sent by God to help her through tough times. And... her job didn't end when Granny died. She's helped Ms. Madeline and me through some pretty crazy stuff...and tonight is no exception.

With Elsie settled in her spot for the night, I pick Granny's Bible up and read Revelation 7:17. I run my fingers over her handwriting beside the verse...*Stand on the promise*...and a few tears fall.

"Granny," I say. "This one's *over the top*. I don't know how much of this stuff you knew...but... man...it's sure a lot to take in at once. You always told me God wouldn't let anything come my way that He wouldn't give me the strength to walk through.

I'm trying to believe that, but it's too much...way too much. My heart feels like someone's shoved a sword right through it. It's bleeding big time, Granny. But you said...*stand on the promise*...so that's what I'll do... **stand on the promise**."

My body heaves as uncontrollable sobs take over. I'm not sure what's worse, the facts I just found out, or the way they were literally thrown at me. I pound my fist into my pillow crying out for God's comfort.

As I roll over I hear click...click...click. Elsie's toenails are making contact with the hardwood floor. Here she comes...round hound to the rescue!

"Elsie girl...it's ok. I'm going to be ok. God's got me." I lean over and snuggle my face into her neck. "Thanks my angel friend...thanks my little round hound." I ruffle her ears reassuring her and myself that I really will be ok.

Granny taught me we can't change the past, but we can allow the past to change us. It can make us bitter or better...the *choice* is ours, she said.

I thought that was a crock until I came to my senses and got a grip on life. Not that I know much now, but I sure do know a lot more than when I was out there running around getting into some pretty bad stuff.

I'm standing on the promise in Revelation 7:17 that there will be no more tears, or sorrow, or any such thing some day. It doesn't look like that right now, so that's where *faith* comes in. *I've got to believe it no matter what is going on.*

Here's the promise. Write it out on the lines following:

Revelation 7:17:

For the Lamb who is in the midst of the throne will shepherd them and lead them to living fountains of waters, And God will wipe away every tear from their eyes.

_____

_____

_____

I *choose* to wake up every morning and go to sleep every night thinking about that promise. I receive hope and peace when I dwell on it, and not what's going on.

In other words, *I choose to believe…someday, this too, shall pass…there is a time coming when I will no longer experience rejection, pain, tears, or sorrow.*

Even though our situations do not look promising or joyful, we can experience joy, peace, and hope *in the midst of them.* Granny taught me to *look at Jesus* at all times and not what is going on around me. She taught me to *believe God's promises* and *stand on them no matter what.*

As I *look to Jesus* during the tough times, I receive comfort, hope, and peace. I may not understand why things are happening the way they are, but if I keep focused on Him…

<u>*I will be able to function from a place of peace instead of turmoil.*</u>

I must believe the promises of God to combat the inner volcano. *I must take His word and allow it to swallow up the facts of my life. In this world we will have trials and tribulation.* That is what Jesus said. He also said He has overcome this world and we can have *peace in the midst of our trials.*

Here, I'll show you. It's in John 16:33. Write it out on the lines following:

These things I have spoken to you, that in Me you may have peace. In the world you will have tribulation; but be of good cheer, I have overcome the world.

_____

_____

_____

My mind is doing overtime. One half of it is *meditating on God's promises* and the other is *rehearsing the events of this evening*...Elsie barking her head off, the squealing tires as the violators speed away, the crashing sound as the bottle busted the front window, and Ms. Madeline's sobbing.

My memory's fresh and raw. The scene is only hours old. I see myself walking into Granny's living room. Ms. Madeline's on the floor weeping over the broken bottle and the newspaper articles. I pick up the article about my parents...

I feel the *inner volcano* stir as my *stomach reacts* to the sounds and sights of this runaway movie. I lurch forward with clenched fists and my teeth start to grind. My heart starts pounding, and, in a flash, I am up pacing the floor.

Elsie stirs and whimpers. She's the calming factor in the room. I steady myself on Granny's dresser and walk toward Elsie. I sit beside her and she looks up.

I'm shaking and tears are released like a pent up dam. I don't know if they are tears of anger or hurt. They could be tears of frustration or exhaustion. I just don't know. At any rate, Elsie is right beside me. This little dog *is* a gift from God. She *is* a ministering angel sent to minister to my broken heart. Surely God created these animals to help calm our crazy world.

I reach for Elsie and bury my face in her neck. She squirms to accommodate my position and gives me her unconditional love. She licks the side of my face and catches one of my tears on her tongue.

Yes, at this moment, she is a ministering angel.

I rest my head in her neck for a few minutes and rub her back. She is content to let me do what I need to do until I gather myself together enough to get back up.

A gentle, compassionate voice enters my space and I hear four life-changing words...*Alex...it's decision time.*

I know that voice. I've heard it for years. It's Granny in my heart telling me I have a decision to make.

When something traumatic happens to us, our nature is to rehearse the scene over and over in our mind. If we do not process the event Jesus' way, it lingers inside our *dormant volcano* waiting to attach itself to something else and *trigger* an *eruption*.

What do I need to do with each scene as it comes to mind? I need to give it to God. It's His to take care of. *It's my job to stand on His promises.*

I cannot change what happened. What I can change is how I process it and my reactions to it.

I am reminded of a **choice** God gave His people in Deuteronomy. Let's read it together and write it out below:

Deuteronomy 30:19-20:

"…I have set before you life and death, blessing and cursing: therefore choose life, that both you and your descendants may live; that you may love the Lord your God, that you may obey His voice, and that you may cling to Him, for He is your life and the length of your days; and that you may dwell in the land which the Lord swore to your fathers, to Abraham, Isaac, and Jacob, to give them."

_____

_____

_____

_____

_____

We can *choose* to feed the volcano or not. We can *choose* to allow our minds to play the movie over and over or not. We can *choose* to allow the *rejection* to *find root* in our hearts and stir up the volcano or not. It is **our choice**.

During the *night season* when we feel *rejected* to the point of no return, we are faced with these *choices*. If we *choose* to take the *easy way out* and allow the volcano to *erupt*, its lava will leave destruction everywhere it goes. It will destroy relationships, hopes, and dreams. It will cause loss of possessions, jobs, and at times, life itself. *Choosing* the easy way out is *choosing death*.

On the other hand, we can *choose life*. We can *choose* to *combat* the volcano with the *truth that God reveals to us*. We can *choose* to *combat* the *volcano* with the *simplicity of the knowledge of who we are in Christ*. We can *choose* to *combat evil* with *good*. We can *choose life over death*. **It is our choice**.

Conquering the *night season* is one of the toughest things to do in life. It is at night when all *hell breaks loose*, so to speak. Did you ever wonder why bars and nightclubs are *dark?* Many don't have windows...and if they do...most of the time they're covered up. No one can see in, and no one can see out.

During the *night season* it is hard to walk by faith and not by sight. Everything in our life and situation tells us that we are unloved, forgotten, and left to suffer alone. We question everything and everyone...sometimes even God.

We have trouble processing our unexpected traumatic events. It is a time when we are most vulnerable to deception from the devil. He lives and works in darkness. He thrives on the negative and glories in our destruction. He uses the night seasons of our lives to try to destroy us.

Just like a bar or nightclub, our *night seasons* create an atmosphere of darkness. It is a time when no one can see in...and we cannot see out. It is a time where we sit alone on the barstool of life drinking shot after shot of discouragement, disappointment, disillusionment, and despair. If we do not rise from this place, we will succumb to the ultimate intoxication...*defeat which leads to destruction*.

Feeling defeated is a place of hopelessness and extreme darkness.

It is a *negative* place, and it's where the devil wants us to *hang out*. He is the owner and bartender of this place of unlimited shots of darkness. His shelves are stocked with bottles full of intoxicating gloom ready to pour. Discouragement, disappointment, disillusionment, and despair are some of what he pours. If he can get us to sit and drink shot after shot during our *night season*, he will have us where he wants us...intoxicated and paralyzed.

WE THEN BECOME PREY TO HIS DEADLY SOLUTION OF...

...DEFEAT LEADING TO DESTRUCTION.

Nothing makes a person weaker than *feeling defeated.* If we do not rise from the barstool and run out of the bar, he will keep *pouring defeat* into our glasses. *We must not allow that.* Two things we must be aware of during our *night seasons*:

> 1. <u>**Walking in defeat is walking the path toward destruction.**</u>
>
> 2. <u>**The devil's main goal during our night season is to destroy us.**</u>

Let's read about this in the Life Recovery Bible...John 10:10 and write it out:

The thief's purpose is to steal and kill and destroy... (Note...the thief is the devil)

_____

Fill in the blanks:

The devil's purpose is to_____, _____, and_____.

Two things we must be aware of during our *night seasons are*:

> 1. _____.
>
> 2. _____.

During our *night season*, we may be lured by the voices of <u>reason, self-preservation, self-defense,</u> <u>self-pity, anger, bitterness, rage, revenge</u>, or any <u>other voice of darkness</u> to follow the devil's path of *defeat leading to destruction.*

They invite us to his *Night Club* where he has *disguised himself* as one who cares and is willing to listen. He places our names on a barstool and *lures us* into accepting his *first shot of darkness.* "Come...sit." He says. "I've got some good stuff here. It'll numb your pain and help you cope." In our weakened state, we succumb to his invitation and pull up a seat.

He pours the <u>*voice of reason*</u> into an empty glass, and hands it to us. In our agony, we gulp it down all at once. A wide-screen TV with a DVD player hangs from the ceiling. He grins as he reaches for a movie, slides it in, and turns up the volume. As the first scene unfolds, we gasp for air! Flashbacks of horror threaten to consume us as we witness events from our past. "Get revenge!" He shouts. "Look at what happened to you!" He pushes the replay button again and again and we feel as though we will go mad. We hold our head in our hands willing it to stop, but we are powerless to do anything because of our weakened state.

He laughs at our inability to make the movie stop, and reaches for a different bottle. He pours a couple shots of _self-preservation_ and _self-defense_. We gladly gulp some more. "Go tell somebody what happened, you'll feel better. As a matter of fact, tell as many people as you can...the more the better. That'll surely help."

Yeah. We think. _That makes sense. I'll tell so and so...and...so and so...and that'll make me feel better._

We find everybody we can to share our traumatic experience with, but come away disappointed and disillusioned because people really don't understand. We are in worse shape than we were at the beginning because the _spirit of rejection_ arises and _lies to us,_ telling us they really _don't care._

We return to the bar and pull up a seat hoping for some _sympathy._ The devil senses our disappointment. His smile is as big as ever. "I'm so sorry...you poor thing...here have another shot. This one's sure to help." He grabs another bottle from his endless variety of dark drinks, and we see _self-pity_ in big bold letters. We down another shot and ask for more. We sit for hours on end gladly consuming this _deadly liquid_ unaware of its effect on us.

With blurred vision, we watch as he pulls four empty shot glasses from under the bar and lines them up in front of us. He fills them from four unmarked bottles, pours them all into one glass, and says, "Drink this...it's _the bomb!!!_"

We drink the _bitter solution_ but have no idea it is _bitter._ It is _tasteless_ because we are _numb._ He is _very pleased._ **We are drinking poison and we don't know it.**

He carefully places the four bottles back on the shelf and proudly displays them. Through our blurred vision, we read ..._Anger_..._Bitterness_..._Rage_..._Revenge_.

We pass out and hit the floor. We have entered his _path of defeat leading to destruction._

BUT ...THIS DOES NOT HAVE TO HAPPEN!!!!

This story came from one of Granny's study books. I really like it because it speaks my language. She had a way about writing that I could relate to. I think they call it allegory or something like that.

Anyhow, I was drinking all that bitterness and anger and stuff, and was feeling pretty bad. I couldn't shake it and no matter what I tried. I always went back to my *stinkin' thinkin'* and *poison drinkin'*.

Every time I feel myself entering that *dark place*, I think about this story. It's helped me recognize what the devil is trying to do, and gets me ticked off (in the right way) *just enough* to find out how to beat him at his game.

Granny sent me a worksheet along with the story. I want to share it with you. It is pretty simple. If you do it truthfully, I believe it will *change* the way you *respond* to things during your *night season*.

Let's start by making some declarations. This is called *speaking light* into the *darkness* of our *night season*.

Speak out loud, if you can, and write the declarations on the lines provided:

I'm tired of my stinkin' thinkin' and my poison drinkin'.

_____

I'm tired of drinkin' the devil's shots of intoxicating gloom, and heading for *destruction*.

_____

I want to *walk away* from the *bar of dark despair* and *death*, and *sit* at the *King's table* of *light* and *life*.

_____

I want to be a *drinker of light* and *life* instead of *darkness* and *destruction*.

_____

I want to *become victorious* instead of a *victim* in my *night season*!

Personal notes:

_____

_____

_____

_____

_____

_____

_____

_____

_____

_____

CONQUERING OUR NIGHT SEASON
JESUS' WAY

STEP 1: RECOGNIZE THE NIGHT SEASON FOR WHAT IT IS...A SEASON

What do you think of when you read the word...*season*? Do you think of Spring, Summer, Fall, and Winter? Do you think of hunting season, hay fever season, mating season, or rainy season?

Whatever comes to mind when we read the word...*season*, we must agree it is associated with a *period of time*. It begins and it ends.

The worksheet we are about to do is associated with our *spiritual night season*.

Let's start by *defining* our *spiritual night season*...

A *spiritual night season* is a *period of time* where we are *engulfed in darkness* and *our spirits are fighting for light*. It is a time when we *walk by faith* and *not by sight*. It is a time when we trust an unseen God when our circumstances tell us not to.

It is a time when, by faith, we grasp His outstretched hand, stand on His promises, and trust Him to show us the way out.

In your own words define *spiritual night season*:

_____

_____

Fill in the blanks:

My *spiritual night season* is a _____ of time. It has a_____
and it has an _____. It is only a period of_____.
It will _____last forever. It is a time when, **by faith**, I _____His outstretched hand,
_____on His promises, and _____Him to show me the way out.

TO SURVIVE THE NIGHT SEASON, <u>WE MUST BY FAITH</u>, GRASP HIS HAND, STAND ON HIS PROMISES, AND TRUST HIM TO SHOW US THE WAY OUT.

STEP 2: EXPOSING THE NIGHT SEASON'S SHOTS OF DARKNESS

In order to walk through our *night seasons* in *victory*, we must *expose the work of the devil* during these times of *testing* and *trials*. *We must refuse to drink his intoxicating shots of darkness* and **choose** *to walk by faith and not by sight*.

It is the wise soldier who knows his enemy and how he operates. He wages war with knowledge of his enemy's tactics. He does not take lightly his enemy's ability to strategize *but* **prepares for victory** *by* **becoming skillful** *with the weapons at his disposal*.

This is what we are doing as we work through this short exercise. We are *exposing the enemy's tactics* during our *night season* so that we aren't blindsided by him and fall during battle.

On the lines below, list some of the *shots of darkness* we discussed earlier, adding any you feel you have experienced that we have not discussed.

_____

_____

_____

_____

_____

_____

_____

_____

_____

Complete the following sentences: (Hint: refer back to Granny's story about the devil's bar on pages 88-90. You will probably find the answers underlined in the story!)

Think about each sentence as you complete it and how it *relates to your life*.

Our *night seasons* create an atmosphere of d_____.

The devil lives and works in d_____.

The devil thrives on the n_____ and glories in our d_____ .

Being defeated is a place of hopelessness and_____.

The devil's shelves are full of intoxicating g_____.

Nothing makes a person weaker than feeling d_____.

Defeat leads to _____.

The devil's main goal during our night season is _____.

Some of the voices we may be enticed with during our night season to drink the shots of darkness are:

Voice of Reason_____

Self-_____

Self-_____

Self-_____

A_____

B_____

R_____

R_____

As we *expose* the devil's schemes during our *night season*, we are **waging war** from **the place of victory**. We will *not succumb* to his tactics and become prey for him to devour **because we have brought his darkness out into the light**.

He will *not be able* to blindside us and cause us to fall in battle because we *recognize him for what he is*...a defeated enemy!

We will *be aware* when his *voices of reason* try to lure us to his table of defeat and tempt us to drink more darkness. We *will refuse* his drinks and walk through the *night season* with *light in our hearts*.

Personal notes:

_____

_____

_____

_____

STEP 3: RECOGNIZE OUR NIGHT SEASON AS A PATH WE DON'T WALK ALONE.

What do you think of when you read the word...*path*? Do you think of something you cut through brush in the woods? Are you a lover of horses and think of a trail to ride? Are you the analytical type and think of a course of action to take? Do you think of bicyclists as they ride on their *designated paths* through a park?

Whatever we think of when we read the word...*path*, we must agree that a _path is a designated route constructed for someone or something to get from one place to another_.

We learned in the previous exercise that our *spiritual night season* is just a season. It has a beginning and an end.

In this exercise, we will learn that, even though it may feel like it, we are never alone during our *night season*. _We will learn it is a path we do not walk alone._

Let's begin by writing out the definition of: *the path during my night season*:

The path set before me during my night season is a designated route constructed to help me get from one place to another. I will learn to walk by faith and not by sight.

_____

_____

Go back to where you wrote about a painful experience in your life and answer the following questions:

1. Did you feel alone while going through the painful experience?

   _____

2. Do you still feel pain when you think about the experience?

   _____

3. Do you believe God cares about how you feel?

_____

During our *night season* we may feel *isolated* and *alone*. We may feel like no one understands or cares. We don't know where to turn or what to do. There is nowhere to hide because we can't run away from the thing that has caused us so much pain.

What *then* do we do? To *whom* can we turn? *How* do we navigate *this path* and *move on* when all evidence indicates we are stuck in the dark?

How do we *walk by faith* and not *by sight* when *we don't understand*?

Once again we must turn to the *Word of God, the Bible,* for our answers. Read the following verses and write them out:

John 6:63: (Jesus is speaking in this verse)

It is the Spirit who gives life; the flesh profits nothing. The words that I speak to you are spirit, and they are life.

_____
_____
_____

Psalm 119:105

Your word is a lamp to my feet and a light to my path.

_____

What do John 6:63 and Psalm 119:105 mean to you when you are hurting?

_____
_____
_____
_____

When we are walking through a *traumatic experience* and *feel darkness closing in*, there is only one place to turn. It is to the Word of God, the Bible.

We may have friends and family members who try to listen and help, but God is the only One who can heal the deep wounds in our souls. Only God can set us free from the *bitterness*, *anger*, and *rage* that threatens to destroy us and everyone in our path. He is the only One who can *extinguish the volcano within* and cause it to become *inactive*.

No one but God can shine light into our spiritual night season.

Write Psalm 119:105 out again:

Your word is a lamp to my feet and a light to my path.

Every morning we wake up during our *night season*, we have a **choice** to make. We can **choose** to enter the devil's bar and drink his poison, or, we can **choose** to sit at the King's table and drink His new wine.

Let's read Ephesians 5:18-20 from the Life Recovery Bible:

Don't be drunk with wine, because that will ruin your life. Instead, be filled with the Holy Spirit, singing psalms and hymns and spiritual songs among yourselves, and making music to the Lord in your hearts. And give thanks for everything to God the Father in the Name of our Lord Jesus Christ.

Explain in your own words what Ephesians 5:18-20 would mean to you during a *night season* of *testing* and *trial*:

_____

_____

_____

_____

_____

What are the two **choices** we have when we are walking a *night season path*?

    1. **Choose** to enter the devil's _____ and drink_____.

    or

    2. **Choose** to sit at _____ and drink_____.

We have already discussed in detail what happens when we enter the devil's bar and drink his poison. We become intoxicated with darkness and unable to function. We end up passing out and are found incapacitated...

BUT IT DOESN'T HAVE TO END THERE!!!

Jesus sees us in our time of need and *always has compassion* on us. He looks at us passed out on the floor *unable to move* and in *deep pain*. He hovers over us protecting us, and all the while:

He is speaking life and light into our place of death and darkness.

Let's read Ezekiel 16:4-14 from the Life Recovery Bible. It is a beautiful story of how God brought His people out of *their* night season.

As you read the story, read it as *your story*…

On the day you were born, no one cared about you. Your umbilical cord was not cut, and you were never washed, rubbed with salt, and wrapped in cloth. No one had the slightest interest in you; no one pitied you or cared for you.

On the day you were born, you were unwanted, dumped in a field and left to die. But I came by and saw you there, helplessly kicking about in your own blood. As you lay there, I said, 'Live!' And I helped you to thrive like a plant in the field. You grew up and became a beautiful jewel. Your breasts became full, and your body hair grew, but you were still naked.

And when I passed by again, I saw that you were old enough for love. So I wrapped my cloak around you to cover your nakedness and declared my marriage vows. I made a covenant with you, says the Sovereign Lord, and you became mine.

Then I bathed you and washed off your blood, and I rubbed fragrant oils into your skin. I gave you expensive clothing of fine linen and silk, beautifully embroidered, and sandals made of fine goatskin leather. I gave you lovely jewelry, bracelets, beautiful necklaces, a ring for your nose, earrings for your ears, and a lovely crown for your head. And so you were adorned with gold and silver. Your clothes were made of fine linen and were beautifully embroidered. You ate the finest foods-choice flour, honey, and olive oil-and became more beautiful than ever. You looked like a queen, and so you were! Your fame soon spread throughout the world because of your beauty. I dressed you in my splendor and perfected your beauty, says the Sovereign Lord.

This *rags-to-riches* story is a picture of what God wants to do for us when we find ourselves in a *desperate night season*. His plan is to pick us up, clean us off, and show His glory through our lives. This brings us *hope* and *courage* to **choose** to *leave the devil's bar* and *enter the King's palace*.

Read Ezekiel 16:4-14 again.

Can you relate to the events in the story? Write your thoughts below:

_____

_____

_____

_____

_____

_____

We aren't told how long it took for God to do His work in this story. What we are told, however, are *the facts of a very traumatic chain of events that could have produced fertile ground for the spirit of rejection to take root*.

The Bible says they were *helplessly kicking about in their own blood. God saw this helpless situation and arrived on the scene ready to make major changes*.

Where are you today? What things have happened in your life to make you feel like this story in Ezekiel was written about you?

Do you believe God sees your helpless situation and has already arrived on the scene ready to make major changes? Why or why not?

_____

_____

_____

Re-Read Ezekiel 16:4-14 often for hope in your desperate-helpless night season!

Let's revisit and rewrite Psalm 119:105:

Your word is a lamp to my feet and a light to my path.

_____

We have established the fact that God can and does intervene in *seemingly helpless situations* and *causes major changes to happen*. In our story in Ezekiel, we find, from the beginning, *rejection-filled* words such as:

_____

1. No one cared for you.

2. You were never washed.

3. No one had the slightest interest in you.

4. No one pitied you or cared for you.

5. You were unwanted.

6. You were left in a field to die.

In the midst of this *dark existence*, we read some *powerful, life-giving words*:

> **But** *I came by and* **saw** *you there, helplessly kicking about in your own blood. As you lay here, I said,* '**Live!**' (Ezekiel 16:6)

God saw the helpless situation and spoke life into it!

In the midst of speaking life into the situation, God stated the *facts*: You were unwanted...You were left in a field to die...No one cared about you... No one pitied you...They were the *facts* and He did not deny them.

Receiving emotional healing does not come from having the ability to deny things the way they are. It does not come with the ability to ignore or pretend the *facts* are not evident. It is not received by the ability to shove *facts* so far deep within ourselves they cannot affect us.

Receiving emotional healing comes from *facing the facts* and *hearing God say...*

BUT...LIVE!

CHAPTER 9
Speaking Life Into Dead Facts

I hear a light tap on my door. "Alex?"

"Yes, Ms. Madeline?"

"I saw your light's still on and wondered if you knew what time it is. Remember, we have to get going early tomorrow..."

"Yeah...I know. I'm just going through some of Granny's letters and worksheets. I'll hit the sack after I'm done."

"We can cancel the publishing appointment in the morning, if you want."

"That might not be a bad idea. I'm really not in to all the corporate nonsense after what's happened tonight. It's too exhausting. I'm afraid I might blow up again. I'm just not too stable right now."

"I agree...you get a good night's sleep and I'll call the publishing house in the morning. I won't wake you."

"Thanks, Ms. Madeline."

I hear her light footsteps head down the hall and Elsie stirring. I find a worksheet on *speaking life into dead facts*. I think it might help me...

SPEAKING LIFE INTO DEAD FACTS...
FACTS ENSLAVE US,
TRUTH SETS US FREE
By Granny G.

Hey! Why don't you do Granny's worksheet *with* me? I'm going to use this latest *traumatic event* that I titled, "*Flying Bottle of Crap*," to do the worksheet. Pick one of *your own traumatic events* and use it to complete this exercise.

Take the event that has caused you so much pain and list some of the facts that *trigger the pain*:

The facts of My (Alex's) traumatic event:

Someone invaded my privacy and threw a bottle through my living room window. I found stuff about my parents that reminded me that they left me. My dad was killed while driving drunk. My mom was accused of having an affair, and walked out on me when I was just a kid. I feel abandoned, unwanted, neglected, and worthless. What kind of horrible kid was I that my mom just walked out on me? Why did my dad drink so much? Was I not worth living for?

The facts of your traumatic event: _____

_____

_____

_____

_____

_____

_____

During this study, we have been learning about the *spirit of rejection*, and how it becomes a *controlling spirit* that *causes us to become a volcano ready to erupt* at any minute. Most hurts and deep wounds we experience have their **root** in this spirit.

On the following lines explain how the *spirit of rejection* has caused you so much pain in this particular situation:

My (Alex) explanation of how the *spirit of rejection* has caused me pain tonight...

I feel rejected by everybody right now. Granny's gone...she died on me when I was in the *County*. Mamma and daddy were never in my life. They drank and drugged until they were completely gone. Elsie, my little sister was killed and left me. These cats that we're trying to get to publish Granny's work reject us day after day. I just feel like nothing in my life is worth anything. Nobody wanted to stick around for me. Who knows why these jerks went to the trouble to copy all that crap in the newspapers and throw it through our window…what kind of craziness is that? Why did they *get off* on doing that? Where are You, God? And…all the years I spent locked up…talk about *REJECTION*, capital *R*. You *NEVER* knew who your friends were, and then you didn't even trust yourself. REJECT!!! Yeah…put me in a cage like an animal… no…most animals are treated better. No sir…right now I feel pretty *rejected* and *ticked off* about *everything*!

Your explanation of how the *spirit of rejection* has caused you so much pain:

_____

_____

_____

_____

_____

_____

_____

_____

_____

_____

_____

_____

_____

_____

_____

_____

When we continue to *experience rejection* and *do not process it Jesus' way*, we risk becoming a *volcano ready to erupt*. We find ourselves *hanging out* in the *devil's bar* where he continues to gladly pour us shots of disappointment, discouragement, and defeat.

Remember…***BUT LIVE***? These two life-giving words find their way through our darkness to *bring us hope* if we **choose** to listen.

It is because God refuses to allow us to be overcome, that we are able to survive the night season as we hear Him say LIVE in the midst of our pain.

On the following lines, write something that *contradicts the facts* in the event you just wrote about…Remember *truth trumps facts*. The Bible is *truth*. Then find some promises in the Bible that *bring light into the darkness* of this event. Ask God to help you. A concordance is a great help in doing this exercise. You can look up a word and find all the verses that have that particular word in it. I looked up *fatherless* to find mine. Here is *the truth that* I found in the Bible that *trump the facts* of my *traumatic event*...

I am a child of God even though my parents aren't here for me. I have a heavenly Father even though I don't have an earthly father. God cares about me because I am parentless. God promises to help me because I am fatherless. I am worth everything to God...He sent Jesus to die for me. I have great worth. I am loved.

Psalm 10:14	You are the helper of the fatherless.
Psalm 146:9	He relieves the fatherless and widow;
Hosea 14:3	"...For in You the fatherless find mercy."
Jeremiah 31:3	"Yes, I have loved you with an everlasting love..."
John 3:16	"For God so loved the world (Alex)..."
John 14: 18	"I will not leave you orphans. I will come to you".

On the following lines, write the truth that *you* found in the Bible that *trump the facts* of *your* traumatic event...

_____

_____

_____

_____

_____

_____

_____

_____

We must come to an understanding of the <u>difference</u> between <u>facts</u> and <u>truth</u> in order to *survive* our *night season*. When every fact points to the assumption that God is nowhere to be found, could care less about us, or what we are going through, **we must hold onto truth**.

Truth is an *anchor* in the *violent storm* of our *night season*. Truth is everlasting from before the beginning of time. Truth will rule the nations and cause the *night season* to *be bearable...*

TRUTH IS GOD'S WORD AND TRUTH IS JESUS

Consider and write out the following verses:

John 14:6:

Jesus said to him, "I am the way, the truth, and the life..."

John 17: 17:

Sanctify them by Your truth. Your word is truth.

2 Corinthians 5:7

For we walk by faith, not by sight.

During our *night season*, we will have to *walk by faith* and *not by sight*. For the promises of God seem far away and the *facts scream* for our attention.

Facts call us to believe what we see. Faith calls us to believe what we can't see.

It is in the desperate night season where *faith* is *tested* by *facts*. We must continue to *hang onto God's word* in *faith* in order to weather the storm. We must *refuse* to let facts rule our actions and reactions. We must *refuse* to allow the *spirit of rejection* to get hold of us during our *night season.*

God is good. God is love. God is perfect. People are not. People hurt people. Whatever has caused us to experience emotional pain, it is during the *night season* we are given the free will to *choose* which path we take.

Are we going to stay on the path that leads to destruction, gulping down endless shots of negativity and despair? Or, are we going to *choose* the path that leads to light and life, even during the darkest days of our lives?

The *choice* is ours. It's always ours.

Which path will you *choose?*

Alex's Personal notes:

Jesus…I love You and know You always do what's best for me. You're always with me. I know You've got my back because You wore all the stripes for my healing on Yours. I know from reading the Bible that I will never experience all the pain You went through. I know You are here and willing to help me. I don't understand why all this is happening now, but I trust You. I am *not* going to *focus on the facts* of this evening, *but on Your word*. I thank You for Your word! ***I thank You that Your Word trumps the facts!*** I rest in Your love. Your beloved child…Alex.

Personal notes:

_____

_____

_____

_____

_____

_____

_____

_____

_____

CHAPTER 10
Forgiving the Facts

I gently lay Granny's worn out, tattered Bible on the nightstand and turn out the light. It has been an exhausting day, and I'm more than ready to count sheep. I hear Elsie's steady breathing as she has settled down again.

It is such a comfort to have her here in the room. I can't explain it, but if you've ever had a pet, you know what I'm talking about. They can fill a void no human being can. I think it's the combination of them needing us, and us needing them, that makes for such a perfect relationship.

Anyhow, I'm glad Ms. Madeline offered to cancel the meeting at the publishing house. After the run-in I had at Mr. T's, I want to take a break from going to places like that for a while.

I've been copying Granny's stuff and handing it out at *The County* when I volunteer, so it's not like we aren't able to use it. I just know it would be cheaper to print them through a publishing house…I've already checked it out.

Oh well…*got'a leave that in God's hands along with the rest of this crazy night.*

In case you're wondering, they let me go back into *The County* to volunteer since I've been out of the system long enough. It's kind of strange, but exhilarating at the same time. I look forward to my time there every week. I'm hoping to get more time slots, but we've got so many volunteers, that won't happen any time soon.

With thoughts of going into *The County* and sharing what happened tonight, I'm almost asleep. I used to love it when the volunteers came in and taught from their life experience. I know the guys are going to love this one tomorrow, so until then…

"Night…Elsie…"

FORGIVING THE FACTS

During the course of this study, we have established several things:

1. We will have periods of time when we *experience rejection.*

2. The *spirit of rejection* causes *emotional pain* and has the ability to temporarily render us incapable of controlling *anger* and *rage.*

3. If we do not process the emotional pain caused by *rejection* Jesus' way, we will become *volcanoes ready to erupt* at any given moment.

4. *Spiritual night seasons* are a *period of time,* with a beginning and an end.

5. During our *spiritual night season,* God is with us and has made provision to help us along the way.

6. *God's Word* is *truth,* and the *truth* is *more powerful* than *the facts.*

7. *We cannot change the facts,* but we *can choose* how we *react* to them.

During this final segment of our study, we are going to learn how to **tap into** the **power** that *will **give us the ability*** to walk through every night season with dignity, stability, and the ability to render the *inner volcano **extinct**.* This **power** has been given to us by the Spirit of Jesus that resides within every one of His children.

To refresh our memories, we learned that there are 3 stages a volcano can be in.
Fill in the description on the lines provided:

      1. The active stage.   Description_____

      2. The dormant stage.   Description_____

      3. The extinct stage.   Description_____

Our goal as Christians is to live life as Jesus did. He is our example. As we read at the beginning of this study, *Jesus experienced rejection* at every turn in His life. At the end of His life, *He was murdered because of rejection.*

One of the last things Jesus said while He was dying was, "Father, *forgive* them, for they do not know what they do." (Luke 23:34)

Here-in lies the power..."Father, forgive them for they know not what they do."

Isaiah, Chapter 53 tells us Jesus was *despised* and *rejected* by men. He was a man of *sorrows* and *knew much grief.* He was *wounded* for our sins. He was *beaten* in order that *we may know peace.* He was *whipped* so that *we may be healed.*

He didn't defend Himself, but willingly went to the cross so we can be free.

Jesus' power on the cross came from asking God to forgive those who had done Him so much wrong. He was innocent, yet murdered. He was kind, yet despised. He gave up everything for those who would stab Him. He walked among people, healed their diseases, raised their dead loved ones, loved them and loved them some more. Yet, He was *despised* and *rejected, stripped naked* and *left for dead.*

In spite of all that happened to Jesus in His life, at the bitter end He said, "Father forgive them, for they know not what they do."

How about me? How about you? Am I willing to ask God to forgive those who have hurt me so? Are you willing to ask God to forgive those who have hurt you?

Again I say...this is the **power** we have available to us...*forgiveness.* This is the **choice** we have during our *night season.*

To forgive or not to forgive...it is **our choice.**

To forgive or not to forgive... it's our choice.

Jesus *chose* to forgive those who had done Him wrong, but He went one step further. He asked God to forgive them! Am *I willing* to take these two steps in order to *experience victory* during *my* night season? Are *you willing* to take these two steps in order to *experience victory* during *your* night season?

Am *I willing* to *forgive* in order to gain control over my *anger* and *rage?* Are you *willing* to *forgive* in order to gain control over **your** *anger* and *rage?*

Being *willing* is the same as *choosing*.

Victory over the grave was just around the corner for Jesus. It was not immediate, but it was close at hand. *His victory began with forgiveness.* Victory for us over the graves of our night season *begins with forgiveness*.

Victory or defeat during our night season is ours according to what we choose. Forgiveness brings victory…Unforgiveness brings defeat.

WILL YOU CHOOSE FORGIVENESS AND VICTORY TODAY?

List some of the facts of Jesus' life that would cause Him to feel rejected:

_____

_____

_____

What did Jesus do at the end of His life when He experienced the *ultimate rejection*?

_____

What has happened in your life that has caused *you* to *experience rejection*?

_____

_____

_____

_____

_____

Fill in the blanks:

Forgiveness brings me v_____

Unforgiveness brings me d_____

I choose: (check one)

____forgiveness

____unforgiveness

**I choose**: (check one)

____ victory
____ defeat

We have established that Jesus' victory over death and the grave was solidified when He asked God to forgive those who rejected and murdered Him.

Victory during our night season is directly related to us _choosing_ to _forgive_. This may be something we will have to **choose** numerous times before we are completely set free.

Why? Because we have been hanging out in the devil's dark bar drinking his poison for _way too long_. The traumatic event is ingrained in our memory, and he replays the scene every chance he gets.

It's during _movie time_ when _we are faced_ with the _decision_ to **choose** forgiveness. Every time we _choose_ forgiveness, the scene _loses its power over us_ and _dims_.

Eventually, it will fade away.

Again, it's **_our choice_**.

On the lines below write about an event in your life where you know you need to forgive someone and ask Jesus to help you. He knows what you're going through.

_____

_____

_____

_____

Jesus, I come to You as humbly as I know how. This event has caused me so much pain; I know I can't forgive without Your help. I come to You; asking You to help me. I believe You understand where I am coming from and want to help me. I want to _release_ this person/these people from _my anger_ caused by _my pain_. Please _heal the wounds_ in my heart so that I can forgive completely, and live free from the anger that is associated with this event. Every time the memories surface, please help me to forgive again until the event no longer affects me and it fades away. Thank You for hearing my prayer and helping me! I love You, Jesus and trust You to see me through. Your child_____.

I _____ *choose* to forgive_____

*for*_____

_____

Thank You, Jesus for hearing my prayer and helping me to forgive!

Every time you experience a memory that causes you pain, come back to this simple, but powerful exercise. You will be surprised how *choosing to forgive* will cause your *inner volcano* to become *extinct!*

Personal notes:

_____
_____
_____
_____
_____
_____
_____
_____
_____
_____
_____
_____
_____
_____
_____
_____
_____

CHAPTER 11
Favor Follows Forgiveness

I wake to Ms. Madeline tapping on my door. It must be morning because light is shining through the shades.

"Alex…Chaplain Whitmire is on the phone…wants to know if you can come in for the 9am time slot."

I reach over and turn the clock around. It's only 7:30. "Sure, tell him sure."

Elsie is on her feet, wagging her tail. As soon as she hears my voice, she thinks it's time to go outside. I stretch and get up, slowly grabbing Granny's Bible on the way out. Elsie follows me to the door and it appears we've started a new day.

Wonder what's going on at the County that Chaplain Whitmire wants me there early? Maybe somebody cancelled. Oh well, it'll give me the afternoon to get some stuff done around here…

I smell biscuits 'n gravy and smile. Ms. Madeline sure gives it a try, but *no one* does biscuits 'n gravy like Granny. At any rate, I down them like I haven't eaten in days. I finish in record speed, grab my coat and cap from the back of the chair, and head toward the front door.

"I'll see you about noon, Ms. Madeline. You need anything from the store?"

"Nope…we're good." She says.

"K…See ya."

"Alex?"

"Yes, Ms. Madeline?" I pause at the front door.

"You *ever* gonna retire that ball cap? It's seen better days, you know…"

"Ms. Madeline, you *know* Granny gave me this cap the first time she took me over to Schenley Park to try out for Little League! When I realized *my parents* were the *only parents* who weren't there, I wanted to run away and never come back. Granny figured that might happen, so she came prepared. She pulled this here cap out of her duffle bag, handed it to me, and said, "Alex, I know I'm not your daddy, but I could hit a mean homerun in my younger days. You never mind that I'm your Granny. You just get out there on the field and make me the proudest Granny in the whole world!" Ms. Madeline, I made the team that day, and from that day on, I called this here cap my *lucky cap*. Granny wasn't too happy 'bout me calling it that. She said, "Ain't no luck 'bout it, Alex. It's God who made it happen."

I tip my *lucky cap* toward Ms. Madeline and wink. "So, to answer your question, *NO*, I will *never retire* this here cap that *you say* has seen better days! I'm going to write it in my will that whoever buries me; makes sure I'm wearing my *lucky cap*. Or, should I say, to respect Granny's opinion, my "*God who makes things happen cap!*"

Laughter from the kitchen follows me out the front door…

It's less than a half hour ride over to *The County*. Good thing. Granny had to make the trip quite often. I can't believe I'm still alive. I'm sure she wanted to beat the tar out of me more than once. "Quit running Alex," she'd say. "It's only a matter of time and the Good Lord's gonna catch you and make something decent out'a ya."

Well, Granny. All that prayin you did all them years finally paid off. I hope you can see what your Alex's doing now. Yup, I'm driving myself to the County! I'm not in no police car being driven there. And…I'm totin' your Bible, Granny! How 'bout that?

I think you'd be right proud Granny…I think you'd be right proud.

The local TV van's leaving the parking lot as I pull in. I don't pay much attention to it because, after all, we are at *The County*…a news-chaser's heaven…

"Hudson? That you…Hudson?"

I recognize the voice and turn. Officer Delaney is pulling around the corner. We know each other well. He spent quite a bit of time with me, or, should I say, I spent a lot of time *doing time* under his supervision.

"Yes, Sir…Officer Delaney…it's me…Hudson."

"Just checking. You doing well, Hudson? Staying out of trouble?"

"Yes, Sir. Officer, Sir. I'm staying out of trouble."

I head toward the front door with a grin. Big bold letters are etched in the door… *County Detention Center*. Bet he never thought he'd see me back here when I could leave the same day… *and* totin' a Bible…

I sign in and am cleared to go down to the block. Chaplain Whitmire's office is on the way. I tap on his door. "Yes?"

"Chaplain. It's me, Hudson. You wanted to see me?"

"Alex? Mmmm…just a minute."

I hear shuffling and mumbling. *What's going on in there?* Another Officer passes by as I wait. Chaplain Whitmire opens the door.

"C'mon in…Alex."

I enter and am surprised to see an officer standing by on the east side of the room. His arms are folded. He is clearly guarding the guy who is sitting in the chair in front of the Chaplain's desk. The guy's hands are cuffed and his feet are in shackles. He's wearing drab gray prison garb that indicates he's a federal inmate. Sometimes the Feds don't have enough room in their holding facilities so they house some of their inmates at *The County* until their trials. Anyhow, this whole thing is very *strange. What am I doing in here?*

The officer nods and the inmate gets up and slowly turns to face me. I remember those cuffs and shackles…you can't move quickly in any direction. My heart rate escalates and I feel blood rush to my head. Instinctively, without any thought, my fists clench and my teeth grind. I have little control over my physical reactions. This is not good. I fight to keep it together.

Why'd they bring me in here? Are you crazy, Chaplain?

Granny's voice fights for my attention. Actually, it fights for my life. If I lose it and go after him, I'm done. I'll go down the road for good. Because if I get to him…

The battle for my life rages in my mind...

Granny pleads…*Alex! You gotta fogive! Alex! You gotta forgive!*

No way man! Forgive this cat? No way! Go for the throat! He'll never know what hit him. Go on man! He deserves to DIE!

My throat constricts and I'm having a hard time breathing.

Again, somewhere in my mind I hear Granny… *Alex! No! Forgive…choose to forgive…Alex! There's too much at stake. You gotta forgive Alex! Alex! Alex! You gotta forgive!!! Make the right choice, NOW!*

I shake my head to stop the battle and get a grip. He's looking at me with terror in his eyes and backs up against Chaplain Whitmire's desk. The officer is approaching me. Silently, I pray. Not much of a prayer. All I can think of to say is… *Jesus help!* It's enough. My heart rate slows, my fists relax, and my teeth stop grinding.

Chaplain Whitmire senses the tension and says, "You two know each other?"

I say, "Carlucci…"

He says, "Hudson…Alex Hudson."

"YUP…it's me. Long time, no see…eh?"

"Your sister…man…I never meant…"

The officer in charge of Carlucci is *not* too pleased with this exchange and quickly escorts him out of the room. I am eternally thankful. The door slams sounding like every other door slamming in this place and it gives me the creeps. I'm not sure what to do with what just happened.

Chaplain Whitmire apologizes. "Alex…I had no idea…"

"No worries Chaplain, I can handle it."

"I'm here any time you want to talk."

"Thanks, but not right now. I got a lot going on, and I've got to get down to the block. It's almost 9:00. Did you need to see me for something? Ms. Madeline said you called."

"Just wanted to see how you guys were making out with Granny's material. Are we going to have books anytime soon? I'm getting a lot of requests from the inmates for her worksheets."

"Well…not so good. The publishing companies we've gone to haven't been the most receptive. The last one said her material is not *suitable for their readership!* Can you believe it…*not suitable for their readership?* They ought'a be glad she's not around to respond to that nonsense."

Chaplain Whitmire laughs and escorts me out of his office. I head to G-block and he heads to Medical. Before we part ways, I say, "Chaplain, I may take you up on that offer sometime," and silently thank God for helping me *forgive on the spot.* I still have a long way to go as far as Carlucci's concerned, but at least I'm going to G-block today to teach and not live…at least they got him out of the room in time.

The story behind Carlucci is really too long and too complicated to try to explain it here. The Good Lord knows there's enough to fill volumes where he's concerned. Let's just say, for now, it was a miracle I didn't go for his throat, and leave it at that.

Granny told me once, "Alex, sometimes things are better left unsaid." This is probably one of those times.

At any rate, I am walking these halls years later a free man…and, I'm not talking just physically.

It's a pretty good walk down to G-block past the kitchen, medical, the Chief's office, and various other blocks. Every once in a while I run into someone, but for the most part, I'm in the halls alone…that is except for the monitors that hang from the ceiling. Those things give me the creeps too. There's just something about being stared at by someone you can't see that still unnerves me.

Anyhow, I'm gearing up for an awesome time in the block. It's when I have to rely on God alone, our meetings are *over the top.* And, I mean that with the most respect.

You see, when I come in with nothing to give, God does it all. I gave up pre-planned meetings long ago. That's not my style…or, should I say my gift. I am more the *spontaneous type* who likes *go with the spirit,* so to speak. Before I came to Jesus and let God have control of my life, that *was not* a good thing. I would *spontaneously* go with the *wrong spirit* and get myself in big trouble, if you know what I mean.

I've shared a lot of these *spontaneous experiences* to let the guys know they can make it if they'll just humble themselves and do things God's way. I don't sugar coat anything or tell them Jesus is an *instant fix-it* kind of guy we can use to get our own way. But, what I do is, share how God can change a spontaneous hot-head like me and turn him into a life-giving channel of peace and hope. As I walk toward G-block, I ask God to take over the meeting and have His way with us. I ask Him to help me hear the cries of the people, and hear His response to them.

I commit the time in the block to His care, and thank Him for going before me. I ask Him to heal and set free those who will attend, and stand on His promise that He has come to heal the brokenhearted and set the captives free.

I walk with joyful expectation because I know God is with me…

The place is packed. There are orange-suited bodies all over the place. Some are playing cards, some are watching TV, and some get up and walk toward the meeting room when they see me come in. They line up in front of the door waiting for the attending officer to open it.

It is the same scene every time I come in. I never tire of it. It's the most refreshing thing I engage in all week. I admire each one who stands in line waiting for a word from God, and silently pray they will not be disappointed.

It took me a long time when I was *locked up* to become one of them…the hot-head turned humble. It takes humility to admit you need help. It takes much more humility to admit you need God's help.

"Alex!" A chorus of shouts invite me to join them. I receive an OK from the officer and make my way through the line to enter the room.

We have a large group today and it's loud…and I mean *LOUD*. When you're *locked up*, everything is locked up…your body, your spirit, your emotions, and your soul. So, when you are given the opportunity to express yourself in the midst of a church service…well… It tends to get *very loud*.

"Hey! Hey! It sounds like a cackling hen house in here! Hey y'all, I understand the Bible says laughter is good medicine, but can we have some *QUIET* please? I can't hear myself think!"

No one seems to be listening so I make trumpet-sounding noises, and one by one, they settle down. I love it. I love everything about it. I love coming in here. What an honor it is to come in here and spend time with those God wants to heal and set free. What an honor to be able to come in here and share God's love!

Alex Hudson…*the hot-head, pot-head, crack-head, orphan turned Spirit-head, Spirit-fed, Spirit-led*, child of God.

Alex Hudson…the *active volcano ready to erupt at any given moment turned into a powerful, life-giving source.*

Who would have ever thought it? Granny? Yes, Granny for sure. I know she believed it until her dying day.

"OK Guys, whose gonna pray us in? (That's my opening line every time. I want everyone to learn how to pray.)

"I'll do it. Anybody got any requests?" Sal says.

"Yeah…T. J." Kimbo responds.

"Who's T.J." I ask.

"Just came in a couple days ago…don't know much…keeps to himself. Little kid…scared to death. Never been in trouble before. I gave him some of Granny's studies to do and told him to come in. He said maybe."

"OK…let's get goin'…time's a tickin'…" I say.

Sal prays, "Jesus we come to You humbly as we know how. Thank You for loving us and keeping us safe in this here crazy place. Please be with our kids while we're in here and keep them safe. Let them know we love them and miss them. Help us get along in here and be there for each other. Help us respect the officers and let them respect us. Jesus, some days we just don't think we can take it anymore. Please be with us when we feel like that. Help us to love one another and not hurt each other. Please be with everyone who's in medical and make them feel better. For those of us who are waiting to see our lawyers, please bring us news soon. Help us while we're waiting. Help us to want Your will and not ours. Please take away our fear and give us Your peace. Help us to forgive everyone who has hurt us and ask forgiveness from those we have hurt. Thank You for bringing Alex in here and help us hear Your Word. Please be with T.J. as he goes through whatever he is going through. Help him to come in here to learn about Your love. Don't let him spend his time alone. Thank You for hearing our prayer. Amen."

All together we say, *"AMEN."*

"Awesome…Sal," I say. "Now that's not so hard is it?" Everybody laughs. "OK what're we singing today? Who's got a request? Gimme three songs to start."

"How about *Stomp*? I wanna hear *Whitney*. Can we do, *I Can't Give Up Now*? No..wait…how about *My Life is in Your Hands?*

They're firing song titles at me at record speed. We are interrupted by someone coming in and everybody stops talking at once.

I turn, amazed that anyone could quiet this crowd like that. A tiny frame of a person enters and sits near the door. This kid can't be a day older than the cut off for being *locked up* in juvenile.

Instantly, parental instincts kick in and my heart breaks for him. *What's he doing in here? He doesn't look like he'll survive without someone's help. Why is he so little?*

"Sorry to interrupt." His voice shakes.

"No need to be sorry. We were just picking out some songs to sing. Do you want to join us?"

"Yes, thank you." He says.

Our meeting was *over the top*, as I suspected. I told them what happened last night…how I *struggled* with the *pain*, and how *forgiveness* was my *choice*.

We talked about *anger* and *forgiveness*. We talked about the *spirit of rejection* and how the devil uses it to keep us *locked up* in an *emotional prison*.

We talked about the *night season* and how *forgiveness* will help us through. We talked about God being our *greatest need* and how we can come to know Him. We talked about not allowing *unhealed wounds* and *unresolved issues* to cause us to become *an active volcano ready to erupt*.

Most everybody in the room participated and we had good cross-discussions. No one was overbearing, and to my surprise, none of us *hot-heads* got out of hand.

I kept an eye on T.J. during the entire meeting. He didn't participate, but I could *feel* him absorbing everything. I recognized so much of myself in him that it was easy to pray for him. God is amazing.

When the service was over, everyone lined up to thank me for coming in. As they filed out one by one I said, "No, let's thank God for *letting* me come in!"

T.J. lingered behind and said, "Can I talk to you…alone?" We waited until everyone left.

"OK…T.J. What's up?"

"Well, Alex." He would not look me in the eye. "I'm having a real hard time in here. I never been in trouble. The guy's, see, they been sharing your Granny's studies with me. I'm workin' them and they're helpin'. I just wanted to say thank you. I been in church all my life, but I flipped out and almost stabbed my uncle."

He turned and walked out the door.

T.J.'s made a huge impression on me. Here's a kid who's in a very bad place, emotionally. He's ripe for *the path of defeat which leads to destruction.* He needs Godly guidance to help him understand the **root** of his **anger** and **rage**.

I'm more determined than ever to find someone who will publish Granny's stuff. With mixed feelings I pass Medical…*I've got to find somebody!* I make my way through the maze of hallways and press the last call button on the last door.

"Can I help you?" The voice in the voice box says.

"Volunteer leaving…JOO17B." Click…and the door opens.

I exit the housing unit with a combination of determination and sadness… determined, because I have answered God's call to keep pursuing someone to publish Granny's material…and sadness, because no one seems to see the importance of doing so.

Before I sign out for the day, I make my way to the lockers where we have to store what we can't take into the blocks. My coat and cap are there, along with my keys, wallet, and Ms. Madeline's polka dotted umbrella. As I reach in and grab my Schenley Park ball cap, my heart skips a beat. So much has happened since Granny gave me this cap. As I close the locker door I hear Granny's gentle voice… *Alex, it's all about God and what He can do in a person's life no matter what they've done or what they've been through.*

Yeah Granny…You're so right…Look at me…Just look at what God's done with me…

I make my way to the desk where I need to sign out, and a man is standing in front of it talking to an officer. His voice is familiar but I cannot see his face. He is dressed in a three piece suit, and gold cufflinks shine as he lifts his arm to sign the book. He appears to be a visitor and is signing in.

The officer behind the counter hands him a *Visitor's badge* and asks, "Who you hear to see today?"

"T.J Hunnicutt…Sir…G block…Sir."

"I need to see your ID." The officer says.

The man in the three piece suit with the gold cufflinks reaches into his wallet to pull out his license. He is clearly in a hurry and several business cards fall to the floor.

We reach to pick up the cards at the same time, and, as if in a slow-motion movie, we rise at the same time, and our eyes lock.

My heart beat increases, my fists clench, and I have a flashback of T.J. sitting as close to the door as possible during our church service. I hear him asking me if he can talk to me. I *feel* his *guilt* and *shame* as he tells me that he almost stabbed his uncle. I hear him thanking me for Granny's lessons…

"Mr. Hudson." The man in the three piece suit with gold cufflinks says.

"Mr. T…of T's Publishing…" I say.

In this very awkward moment, I am grateful for the officer's interruption. "Excuse me gentlemen…we have others waiting in line."

I take a deep breath. *My only hope now is to instantly forgive…Lord…I* **choose** *to forgive…Help!*"

"Yes…Sir. I won't be a minute. I just have to sign out." I say.

The officer hands me my license and my intention is to fly out the front door as fast as I can and not look back. I am detained by Mr. T's voice.

"Mr. Husdon…may I speak to you privately?"

"Why… Mr. T.? You wanna bash more of Granny's stuff? I thought I made it clear to you when I left your office how I felt." I'm amazed at the control I feel myself under…*instant forgiveness works!*

"Mr. Hudson…may I call you Alex?"

"I suppose so."

"Can we have a seat over there?" He points to the waiting area, and I follow him not sure if I think this is a very good idea.

There is no one waiting at this time so we are alone. He opens a legal-sized binder and pulls out several pieces of yellow legal paper. I recognize this paper. It's what they give you to write letters on when you're locked up in here.

"Alex…I owe you an apology. I owe your friend, Ms. Madeline an apology. And, I owe Granny G. an apology."

"Really?" I point to the pile of yellow paper lying in his lap. "Got anything to do with that?"

"As a matter of fact, it has *everything* to do with it. These are letters I've received from my nephew T.J. He's been *locked up* here for about a week. When you came into my office yesterday, I was still reeling from the fact that he pulled a knife on me and was threatening to kill me."

"Mr. T. He's just a kid, and a walking toothpick at that."

"You don't understand, Alex. It's not that I'm afraid *of him*, it's that I'm afraid *for him*. I had to press charges for his own good. He's been messing around with this girl who's in a gang. I'm pretty sure they're using him to get what they want. He looks so innocent, he can con anyone. But, he's in over his head. I fear for his life. I wouldn't give him money so he threatened me."

"Man, I'm sorry to hear that. I just met T.J. today. It's hard to believe he'd do anything like that. But, then again, most people don't *plan* fits of anger or rage, they *just happen* when something *triggers* them. He must be scared to death."

"Alex, these letters do nothing but praise Granny G's material. T.J. says they're helping him cope and get to the root of his anger and rage. He says he's found God for the first time in his life. Alex, T.J.'s been going to church since he was an infant. I know this for a fact, because I'm the one who's been taking him.

His mother, my sister, was an active user of heroin and they didn't think T.J. would even live. Shortly after he was born, miraculously addiction-free, she died. She did not know who his father was. I intervened and took him in.

When you came into my office, my emotions were raw. It was easier to blow Granny G's stuff off and offend you than to face the fact that someone *I raised* actually *needed it!*"

Now, you could have blown me away with a feather. *Am I dreaming?* "What are you suggesting, Mr. T?" My heart pounds in anticipation.

"Alex, I went to my Board of Directors and spilled my guts. I told them everything. I told them T.J. threatened me. I told them he's in jail and facing some pretty heavy charges. I told them I think Granny G's material is literally keeping him alive.

I gave them his letters to read. By the time they were done, they were in tears. *They* started spilling *their* guts to *me*. It has come out that some of their family members have been in jail or prison before, and some are *still locked up*. It was an amazing time of healing for all of us.

I would like you and Ms. Madeline to meet with us, and bring everything you have of Granny G's. I've asked the Board to review her material, and told them I'm offering you and Ms. Madeline publication for all of it at no cost."

"*VISIT #11...*" The officer behind the desk announces.

"That's me, Alex." Mr. T. stands. "T.J. will be glad I ran into you. I promised him if I didn't see you today, I would get in touch with you somehow."

"Thank you," is all I can say, as I watch Mr. T. pass through security on his way to visit T.J. In a blissful fog of, *Way to go God*, I walk out the front door grinning. I reach into my pocket and pull out a half-eaten bag of Peanut M&Ms. I pop one into my mouth and almost choke as my grinning turns into laughter. *Only God* could pull off something like this…*Less than twenty-four hours ago, I stormed out of that man's office, without a doubt in my mind we would meet again…!!!*

"Granny," I shout as I throw my cap into the air. "What do *you* think about *that?*"

I hear her voice as plain as day, speaking to my spirit…

**"TO GOD BE THE GLORY,
GREAT THINGS
HE HAS DONE.
AMEN."**

CONCLUSION

Thank you for sharing your time with me. I trust this study has helped you as much as it's helped me. You'd be surprised at how much I've learned right along with you.

We've given this study the title,
Help! I'm Locked up and I need Peace...
Extinguishing the volcano within.

God's desire is for us to experience *His peace* in our lives. *His peace* is *not* the absence of *external conflict*, but the *absence of internal conflict*.

I believe *Jesus' peace* came from being in *constant contact with God* and *choosing to forgive* those who hurt Him. We must follow His example in order to *extinguish the volcano within*. Without staying in *constant contact* with God and *choosing to forgive* those who have hurt us, we will continue to experience *inner conflict*, and risk becoming an *active volcano* ready to *erupt* without warning.

It's been an honor and a pleasure sharing my life with you for the short time we've been together. I trust sharing my struggle with *anger* and *rage* has given you the courage to face your own. I believe, as you use what we've learned in this study to recognize what's really going on, you will make the right choices, and…

NO LONGER BE A VOLCANO READY TO ERUPT AT ANY GIVEN MOMENT, CONTROLLED BY THE SPIRIT OF REJECTION…

BUT

A POWERFUL, LIFE-GIVING FORCE, CONTROLLED BY THE SPIRIT OF GOD!!!

God bless you, my friend, as you continue your journey with Him…Alex.

A special note from Ms. Lynn

If you would like answers to some of your questions about Jesus, the Bible, or the Christian life, you may contact me by writing to:

Alex Hudson
c/o Lynn Potter
P.O. Box 11
York, SC 29745

Granny would be pleased to know Madeline and I want to make this book available free of charge to anyone who is locked up. Please fill out the form below and send it to the same address above.

Name_____

Address_____

_____

_____

_____

What are the guidelines for receiving books at the particular institution you are requesting "*Help! I'm Locked Up... and I Need Peace?*" to be sent to?

_____

_____

_____

_____

_____

____   I would like to request a free book.

____   I would like more information on how to sponsor a book.

Please tell me a little about yourself and your interest in this book:

_____

_____

_____

GOD BLESS YOU!

Made in the USA
San Bernardino, CA
04 June 2014